THE NATIONAL GALLERY OF ART

A Guide to CIVILISATION

With an Introduction and Notes by
Richard McLanathan

Prepared for the National Gallery of Art and Published by

TIME LIFE FILMS

New York

The Guide to "Civilisation" is a project of the National Gallery of Art and Time-Life Films. It is an extensive collection of information on the underlying history, the works of art, the people, places, music and terminology in "Civilisation—A Personal View," the thirteen-part film series written and narrated by Kenneth Clark and produced by the British Broadcasting Corporation.

"Civilisation" received its premiere in the United States at the National Gallery of Art, Washington, D.C., which will make this guide available through its extension service. It will also be available through most of the television stations of the Public Broadcasting Service and from Time-Life Films. Prints of the films for sale and rental are distributed in the United States by Time-Life Films. The appearance on public television has been underwritten by Xerox Corporation.

Richard McLanathan, in consultation with the staff of the National Gallery, is the author of the introduction and the supplementary notes for each of the programs. Dr. McLanathan is a frequent lecturer on art in both the United States and Europe and is the author of many books and articles published here and abroad, including *The Pageant of Medieval Art and Life* and *The American Tradition in the Arts*. He has also been a curator of the Museum of Fine Arts in Boston and the director of the Utica Museum of Art.

Research staff for the Guide: Shirley Estabrook, with Patricia Egan, Yvonne Wong, Deborah Trebilcock, Priscilla Flood, Karl Reuling and Don Ferguson.

Contents

Illustrations

Foreword

As Kenneth Clark is quick to point out in the book version of his television series, the title "Civilisation" cannot be construed as describing the necessarily selective approach dictated by the television limitations of thirteen fifty-minute scripts. The subtitle of the series, however, "A Personal View," is descriptive of the series, and is in many ways its greatest strength.

The purpose of the following study guide is not to attempt a definitive summary of what happened in the periods discussed, nor even to indicate all the alternative interpretations that different scholars and specialists might wish to adduce. These functions are better provided in additional readings, some of which have been indicated in the reading list. What it does try to do is to supplement the limitations of the motion picture medium as a form of communication. Time dictates that in a film every image shown cannot be identified and described as well. Although more impressive than any image publishable, a film does not let the viewer turn back, and at the end is darkness.

For this reason, we have attempted to set down some of the salient events, both historical and artistic, to which Lord Clark refers. For a narrative record of the verbal aspects of the film, we would refer the reader to the book, "Civilisation" (New York, Harper & Row, 1969).

In mentioning the things this little book, and the films themselves, cannot provide, may we, from our special vantage, point out one in particular. That is the direct experience of the original work of art, in whatever form. A lifetime of visiting museums, of keeping one's eyes and ears open to the opportunities available, and of relating them to an ever-growing internal framework of what has constituted man's past is, perhaps more even than this guide or the films to which they relate, a little bit of what civilization is all about.

J. Carter Brown
Director
National Gallery of Art

Introduction

The purpose of this brief guide to the "Civilisation" series is to provide background to each of the programs which Lord Clark presents so brilliantly. This background includes the identification of artists and places; definition of art terms; establishment of chronology; illustrations, with maps and diagrams, of important aspects of various periods; suggestions for ways in which the programs, with the assistance of this guide, may be made more useful for the study of the humanities in general, and for the individual viewer who wishes to gain a fuller grasp of the broader subject or some aspect of it. It is our hope that the guide may provide answers to some of the many questions which inevitably must arise when such a vast panorama of time, and such a complex series of developments must be compressed—as has been done by Lord Clark with such distinction—into a visual presentation of only thirteen programs.

The supplementary notes to each program sketch the artistic, cultural and historical context for the basic subjects and periods of that program. They also endeavour to fill some of the chronological gaps, inevitable because of the visual requirements of the medium and the condensation necessitated by the limitation of time. Much, therefore, had to be taken for granted which lies outside the general area of knowledge of all but the specialist. Such information the guide endeavours to supply. And because it is primarily intended for an American audience, the notes also include some major contemporary developments in the New World.

To maintain proper scale, the notes have been made as brief as possible; the programs are, after all, the point. Therefore, drastic omissions were necessary. The selective book list should make it possible to fill these gaps, the time chart should provide a sense of chronological sequence, the maps clarify geographical relationships, the illustrations and diagrams make evident some important engineering and architectural developments more easily shown than described, and the identification of artists and the definitions of art terms provide further clarification. The music used in the programs has also been listed, with the most readily available sources of the recordings noted.

Because of the richness of content of the programs, they lend themselves to a variety of uses, from giving pleasure to the individual viewer to becoming a multi-media teaching medium for courses in the arts and humanities. They can be approached from the point of view of the history of ideas and their expression in literature as well as in the visual arts. They can provide an opportunity for understanding the contributions of the greatest minds of the West, from the beginning of the Middle Ages to yesterday, not only philosophically, but also through all the various forms of creative expression. Since they involve the visual, the aural, and the spoken and written word—all interpreted with conviction and enthusiasm by one of the most knowledgeable and interesting personalities of our day—they provide a unique experience. It is our hope that this brief guide may make that experience yet more satisfying by supplying the means to broaden the potential use of the series, not only in a more formal educational application—whether in a school or college, a museum, in connection with television or other viewing, or whatever—but also in terms of the individual who seeks an understanding, never more important than today, of the world in which he finds himself, the problems he must face and the hopes and possibilities of the future.

Richard McLanathan
Consultant
National Gallery of Art

Kenneth Clark

Kenneth Clark has held so many important positions in the arts and cultural life of Great Britain that he has been called its minister of culture.

He was educated at Winchester and Trinity College, Oxford. After working for two years with Bernard Berenson in Florence, he became Keeper of the Department of Fine Arts at the Ashmolean Museum, Oxford. He was appointed director of the National Gallery, London, in 1934, when he was thirty-one, the youngest man ever to hold that post. He was also Surveyor of The King's Pictures and, during the war years, head of films for the Ministry of Information and later head of films and broadcasts. At the war's end he returned to Oxford as Slade Professor of Fine Arts.

In the 1950's he was chairman of the Arts Council of Great Britain and for three of those years chairman of the Independent Television Authority as well. In 1954 he wrote, directed and appeared in a series of television programs on art and in 1967 conducted a memorable tour of British royal palaces for American television. Even so, Lord Clark prefers to think of himself primarily as a writer and critic. He has published 16 works on art, including *Landscape into Art, Leonardo da Vinci, Piero della Francesca, The Nude, Ruskin, Rembrandt and The Italian Renaissance.*

Kenneth Clark was knighted in 1938, and has recently been given a life peerage. He now bears the title of Lord Clark of Saltwood.

His lectures at Yale, at the National Gallery and at New York University have won him a sizeable American following, but his greatest popular and critical success is the Civilisation series. He has called it his autobiography and has said of it, "The happiest years of my whole life were the years doing these programs, because we all felt we were going somewhere, doing something."

1. The Frozen World

The Dark Ages, with the disintegration of the Roman Empire, the invasions of the Barbarians, the threat of Islam, the achievements of Celtic Christianity in the face of pagan assault and the peril of civilization during the centuries until Charlemagne emerged as the leader of the Franks, renewed ties with Rome and the Byzantine Empire, and re-established the ideal of European unity when he was crowned Holy Roman Emperor in the year 800.

"Civilised man, or so it seems to me, must feel that he consciously looks forward and looks back. And for this he needs a minimum of stability, which was, in Western Europe, first achieved in France, or as it then was, the Kingdom of the Franks. Charlemagne is the first great man of action to emerge from the darkness since the collapse of the Roman world. The old idea that he saved civilisation isn't so far wrong, because it was through him that the Atlantic world re-established contact with the ancient culture of the Mediterranean world."

Three basic elements combined to produce the long and varied arts and culture of the Middle Ages: the heritage of the classical past of Greece and Rome, the exalted mysticism of the Near East where Christianity was born, and the vital traditions of the Barbaric tribes from the north and east. The Greeks, and the Romans after them, had emphasized life in this world. Their idea of an afterlife was a vague, unhappy, ghostlike existence. During the later years of the pre-Christian era a number of what have been called mystery religions were brought from the Near East into the Roman Empire, the worship of such Egyptian deities as Osiris and Isis; of Mithra, a cult into which one was initiated with a ceremony of bull's blood; of the Greek god Dionysos, and many others. All emphasized the existence and importance of life after death, of the continuation of the human soul. They not only proved, as Lord Clark points out, the ennui of the Late Classic world, but also were important in preparing for the coming of Christianity, whose whole basis was faith in immortality, in the continuation of life after death. It was this change which marked the major philosophical distinction between the Classic and Medieval worlds.

The Middle Ages may be considered to have begun about 330 when the Roman Emperor Constantine, having won the sole control of the Roman Empire in a battle just before which he is said to have had a vision of a cross in the sky with the words "by this sign shall you conquer," accepted Christianity as the official religion of the Empire. In this same year Constantine established Constantinople, a new city on the site of Byzantium commanding the Bosporus, as the capital of the Eastern or Byzantine Empire. Suddenly Christianity, an underground cult, whose followers were mostly from the poorer parts of the population, became all-powerful. Suddenly the philosophic outlook of man made the tremendous and significant shift from emphasis on this world to faith in a world to come, an ideal and perfect world of which earthly life was but an imperfect reflection and a preparation, a world entered only by the faithful and through the gates of death. This was the prevailing outlook of the Middle Ages, therefore appropriately called the Age of Faith.

During the same century there were Barbarian invasions of the Empire. Nomadic tribesmen were driven westward by the movements of yet other hordes from the endless steppes and plains of Central Asia. Accustomed to living in camps wherever their herds found grazing and to moving with the seasons, their allegiance was to the tribe rather than to any place. So they came, with their herds, horses and families, relentless warriors worshipping fierce pagan deities, illiterate, but with oral tribal traditions and legends which were eventually recorded in the Icelandic sagas and the Anglo-Saxon epic, *Beowulf*. Their art was of necessity a portable art. It had had its origins centuries earlier in the plains of Central Asia, and was based upon animal and plant forms, abstracted through the years into interlacing elements of decorative and emotional power. It appeared on their sword hilts, daggers, shields and helmets—an art of goldsmith and armorer alike, with precious metals set with brightly colored enamels and gems. The Anglo-Saxon invaders of the British Isles were among these barbaric tribes, as were the much-feared Vikings or Norsemen, who became known as Normans after their conquest in the tenth century of that part of France called after them, Normandy.

From the time of Constantine on, wave after wave of Barbarians swept across the empire, down the Italian peninsula and into Sicily, through Spain into North Africa. They sacked Rome in 455, and, in 476, Odoacer, a barbarian chief, deposed the last emperor of the West. Only the Eastern Empire, centered on Constantinople, remained, as the Barbarians established kingdoms of their own throughout Europe and North Africa.

In the sixth century, the Frankish tribes were consolidated into a state under Clovis, who was converted to Christianity, leading the way to the empire of Charlemagne in the eighth century, and the emergence of Europe from what have been called the Dark Ages. But a great deal that was constructive happened during the Dark Ages. Under the rule of the Eastern Emperor Justinian in the sixth century, Constantinople saw the beginnings of the First Golden Age of Byzantine art. The city became the most beautiful in Christendom, its great church of Santa Sophia still a landmark in world architecture.

In the West, St. Benedict laid down his famous rule for life in the monasteries, which were for centuries islands of culture in war-torn Europe. The Celtic Christian church, established in Ireland by St. Patrick in the fifth century, expanded to influence all Europe, establishing monasteries from Iona, the island which under leadership of St. Columba became its center, to Switzerland, Germany and Italy. Celtic Christian manuscripts, illuminated with the Barbarian interlaced designs, spread throughout Europe. Among them was what has been considered the most beautiful book in the world, the *Book of Kells,* which may have been produced by scribes on Iona itself. So pervasive was Celtic Christianity that Pope Gregory the Great sent St. Augustine, later archbishop of Canterbury, to England to ensure allegiance to Rome. Yet Celtic Christianity, with its mysticism and practicality and its artistic traditions based on a Barbarian past and expressed both in manuscripts and in tall, sculptured, stone crosses, was a profoundly civilizing influence throughout the Christian world, providing outstanding teachers and leaders.

Mohammed was born in Mecca in 570, and the following century saw the rise of the religion he founded, Islam, which united the Arab world and sent its mounted warriors forth to conquer North Africa, Spain, and menace Constantinople itself. In 732 Charles Martel (Charles the Hammer), a Frankish leader, repulsed the Moslem attack on Tours in southern France, preventing an Arab conquest of Europe. In 768 his grandson, Charles, known to history as Charlemagne (Charles the Great) became king of the Franks. With great ability, he established a Frankish kingdom from the Baltic to the Mediterranean, and from Atlantic shores to the Adriatic. When, in 800, Pope Leo III crowned Charlemagne Holy Roman Emperor in old St. Peter's in Rome, the old Roman ideal of a united Europe was revived and future European development assured. Though centuries of strife were to come, the Dark Ages were over.

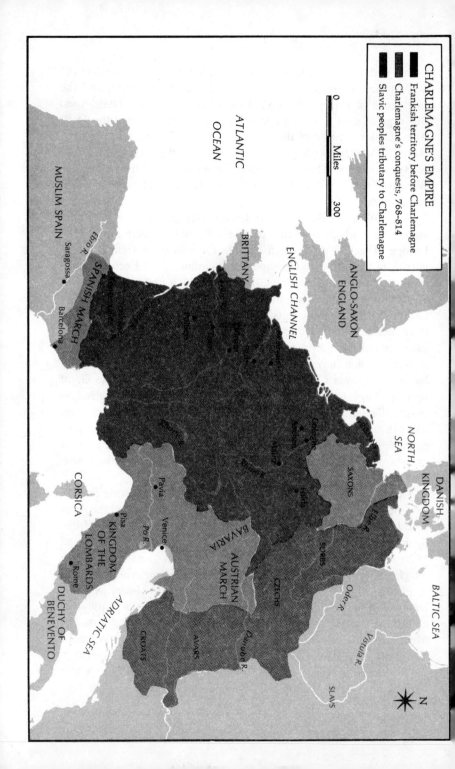

CHARLEMAGNE'S EMPIRE

Frankish territory before Charlemagne

Charlemagne's conquests, 768–814

Slavic peoples tributary to Charlemagne

0   Miles   300

N

ATLANTIC OCEAN

MUSLIM SPAIN

Saragossa

Barcelona

Ebro R.

SPANISH MARCH

BRITTANY

ENGLISH CHANNEL

ANGLO-SAXON ENGLAND

NORTH SEA

DANISH KINGDOM

BALTIC SEA

Loire

Seine

Cologne

Aachen

Main R.

Elbe R.

Oder R.

Vistula R.

SAXONS

SORBS

CZECHS

SLAVS

Pavia

Pisa

Po R.

Venice

KINGDOM OF THE LOMBARDS

CORSICA

Rome

DUCHY OF BENEVENTO

ADRIATIC SEA

BAVARIA

AUSTRIAN MARCH

Danube R.

AVARS

CROATS

Charlemagne and his successors were patrons of the arts and of learning. Though, as was customary among the Franks, his vast empire was divided at his death in 814, the cultural traditions which he had established, enriched by the contributions of Celtic Christianity, flourished. Superb illuminated manuscripts were produced, schools established, monasteries founded, churches built. Also the arts that later ages have termed minor—ivory carvings, goldsmith-work, small-scale objects such as were produced by the Barbarians —became major mediums of artistic expression. Through re-established contact with Byzantium, so long cut off by barbarian hordes, the traditions of the classical past, the writings of the great thinkers of Greece and Rome began to be rediscovered in the West, paving the way for medieval achievements to come. The cultural impetus of the Carolingian period—so-called from Carolus, Charles—continued into the Ottonian period, named for Otto, who revived the Holy Roman Empire with his imperial coronation in 962.

In the ninth century came the Second Golden Age of Byzantine art, whose greatest architectural monument is St. Mark's in Venice (begun 1063), and the reign of Alfred, King of the West Saxons, who started the unification of England and whose patronage marks the beginnings of English literature.

The tenth century found the Arabs firmly established in Spain, where the university city of Cordova was the greatest cultural center in the West. It saw the expansion of the Vikings who not only founded colonies in Greenland, and formed the personal guard of the Byzantine Emperor, but brought the first organized government to the backward Slavic tribes, the beginnings of what was to become the Russian Empire. The Celtic church and that of Rome had joined forces in allegiance to the pope, but the church of the Eastern Empire, centered in Constantinople, chose to remain separate, a division which remains to this day.

The art of the Early Christians, those who lived during the period up through the reign of Constantine, may best be seen in the catacombs around Rome, where they not only buried their dead but also met in secret worship. Theirs was a symbolic art, simple and often crude. The stories of Jonah and the Whale, Noah, and the survival of Daniel in the Lion's Den, for example, stood for the survival of the soul after death through faith. Christ appeared as a young, beardless, Apollo-like young man, and the Virgin, a dignified Roman matron, was often movingly portrayed. The Crucifixion, largely because it represented the form of death reserved for criminals, did not appear in art with any frequency until four centuries later.

With Constantine all was changed. He started building the great basilica of St. Peter's, the largest church in Christendom—its ground plan is larger than a football field—to express the grandeur of the imperial ideal. Its interior was enriched with brilliant mosaics much like those later ones in San Vitale in Ravenna which so impressed Charlemagne and with richly colored marbles such as had earlier decked pagan buildings. Its many altars bore jeweled crosses and reliquaries. No longer was Christianity a poor, underground movement of Jews, slaves and freedmen. It had assumed imperial scale and had become intent upon universal dominion. The way to the monumental achievements of the High Middle Ages—the Romanesque of the 11th century and the Gothic of the 12th through the 14th centuries—was clear.

Works of art as they appear in Program 1

Notre Dame, Paris. Begun 1163, completed in 14th century. Cathedral of Paris, on an island in the Seine River. Facade and nave are Early Gothic in style, transepts and chapels are High Gothic (1250-70). Notable for its fine facade with rose window and three wide portals; also for exterior of east end, with tall flying buttresses above encircling chapels.

Viking prow. Ninth century. British Museum, London.

Frieze, from Parthenon in Athens. c. 440 B.C. Marble, height 43". British Museum, London.

Maison Carrée, Nîmes, France. First century. Roman temple.

Pont du Gard, Nîmes. Aqueduct over River Gard in southern France. Early first century.

Battle of Romans and Barbarians, on the Ludovisi sarcophagus. Early third century. Marble, length 98". Terme Museum, Rome.

Scythian Pot. Fourth century B.C. Gold. Victoria and Albert Museum, London.

Wall Painting, from Villa of the Mysteries, Pompeii. c. 50 B.C.

Musicians and Horsemen, manuscript illumination from an Islamic manuscript of al-Harini. 14th century. Bibliothèque Nationale, Paris.

Early Saints in a Boat, manuscript illumination.

Stone cross and huts, seventh-century monastery on island of Skellig

Michael, western Ireland.

Viking Gold Hoard, sword hilt. c. 825. University Museum of Antiquities, Oslo.

Sutton Hoo Hoard, found in a ceremonial ship buried in Sutton Hoo in Suffolk before 655. British Museum, London. Shown here: purse cover, clasp, coins, shield and other gold objects, decorated with enamel and gems.

Stone cross on Iona. Seventh to ninth centuries. 360 large stone crosses were said to be on the island; nearly all were thrown into the sea during the Reformation.

Lindisfarne Gospels, illuminated manuscript. c. 700. British Museum, London. Shown here: First page of Gospel of St. Matthew and a Cross Page.

Symbol of the Evangelists, manuscript illumination from Gospel book. Tenth century. Episcopal Archives, Trier.

"Imago Hominis" (symbol of St. Matthew), manuscript illumination from *Echternach Gospels.* c. 700. Bibiothèque Nationale, Paris.

Xpi (Greek monogram of Christ), manuscript illumination from Gospel book (Cotton Nero D. IV). Ninth century. British Museum, London.

Book of Kells, manuscript containing four gospels of the New Testament. Early ninth century. Trinity College, Dublin. Shown here: *Xpi* (Greek monogram of Christ) and evangelist portrait from Gospel of St. Matthew.

Gokstad Ship, Viking ship intended for long voyages. Mid-ninth century. Ship Museum, Oslo.

Vikings in Boat, engraved stones. Bunge Museum, Gotland, Sweden.

Oseberg Ship, Viking ship. c. 850. University Museum of Antiquities, Oslo.

Fighting Outside a City; Fighting in a Fort, manuscript illuminations. c. 1150. Trinity College Library, Cambridge, England.

Fighting Men, manuscript illumination from *Book of Maccabees.* Bibliothek van de Rijksuniversiteit, Leyden.

Baptistry of St. Jean. Seventh century. Poitiers.

Charlemagne, reliquary in the form of bust of Charlemagne. c. 1350. Gold with jewels, cameos and other ornament. Cathedral Treasury, Aachen.

Presentation of Bible to Charles the Bald, manuscript illumination, frontispiece of *Vivian Bible.* c. 850. Bibliothèque Nationale, Paris.

Moses with the Tablets of the Law, manuscript illumination from *Moutier-Gandval Bible.* c. 840. British Museum, London.

St. Gregory Dictating, manuscript illumination. c. 983. Municipal Library, Trier.

The Prophet Ezra Writing, manuscript illumination from *Codex Amiatinus.* c. 750. Laurentian Library, Florence.

St. Gregory and Three Scribes, ivory book cover, School of Reichenau. Tenth century. Kunsthistorisches Museum, Vienna.

St. Luke, manuscript page, School of Fulda. Tenth century. University Library, Würzburg.

Page of Script, from *Sacramentary of St. Gregory.* 1586. Bibliothèque Nationale, Paris.

Equestrian Portrait of Charlemagne, from Treasure of Metz. Ninth century. Bronze statuette. Louvre, Paris.

Anthemius of Tralles and Isidorus of Miletus, Church of Santa Sophia. 532-37 A.D. Istanbul, Turkey.

Church of San Vitale, 526-47. Ravenna. Shown here: *Christ with Angels,* apse mosaic; *Sacrifice of Abraham,* wall mosaic; *Emperor Justinian and His Court, Empress Theodora and Her Attendants,* wall mosaics.

Palace Chapel, Aachen. 796-814. Shown here: Gold pulpit with enamel and ivory plaques, consecrated in 805 (commissioned by Charlemagne and built by a Frankish master builder, Odo of Metz); the emperor's stone throne; ornamental wrought iron grille forming balustrade; pilaster capitals.

St. Mark Writing, manuscript illumination from the *Gospel of St. Mark.* Early ninth century. British Museum, London.

Jeweled book cover, with ivory panel of *Death of Virgin,* of *Gospel Book of Otto III.* c. 1000. State Library, Munich.

Ivory plaque from cover of *Prayer Book of Charles the Bald.* Reims, c. 870. Schweizerisches Landesmuseum, Zurich.

Ivory book cover of *Pericopes of Henry II,* School of Reichenau. Tenth century. State Library, Munich.

Cross of Lothair (front). c. 1000. Gold with jewels, cameos and filigree. Cathedral Treasury, Aachen.

Cross of Lothair (back). *Crucifixion.* c. 1000. Silver gilt, engraved. Cathedral Treasury, Aachen.

Crucifixion, one panel of wooden doors on the Church of Santa Sabina, Rome. First half of fifth century.

Gero Crucifix. c. 970-1000. Painted wood, height 6'2". Cathedral, Cologne.

Crucifixion, manuscript illumination from *Ramsey Psalter.* c. 1000.

British Museum, London.

Priests Celebrating the Mass, ivory plaques. Ninth and tenth centuries. Stadt-und Universitätsbibliothek, Frankfurt; Fitzwilliam Museum, Cambridge, England.

2. The Great Thaw

The emergence of medieval Europe in the twelfth century, with the flowering of the Romanesque style, the founding of universities, the spread of monasticism; an age of pilgrimages—to the Holy Land, to Rome and to Santiago de Compostela—and of the building of great churches; of the new view of man of Peter Abelard and the synthesis of Classic and Christian heritages in the great vision of St. Thomas Aquinas. It was a period which saw, under the inspiration of the Abbot Suger, the creation of the Gothic style at the ancient royal abbey of St. Denis, and its flowering at Chartres.

"Chartres is the epitome of the first great awakening in European Civilisation: it is also the bridge between Romanesque and Gothic, between the world of Abelard and the world of St. Thomas Aquinas, the world of restless curiosity and the world of system and order. Great things were to be done in the next three centuries of high Gothic, great feats of construction, both in architecture and thought. But they all rested on the foundations of the 12th century. That was the age which gave European civilisation its impetus. Our intellectual energy, our contact with the great minds of Greece, our ability to move and change, our belief that God may be approached through beauty, our feeling of compassion, our sense of the unity of Christendom—all this, and much more, appeared in those hundred marvellous years between the construction of Cluny and the rebuilding of Chartres."

The 11th century saw the rise of the Seljuk Turks who carried the green banner of the prophet Mohammed to the very gates of Constantinople. Before the end of the century the Normans had taken Sicily from the Moslems, and William, Duke of Normandy, had invaded and conquered England. Just before the end of the century, Pope Urban II called a Council at Clermont in central France to preach the First Crusade to recapture the Holy Places of Christianity from the Moslems, and, in the last year, Godfrey de Bouillon, a powerful French nobleman, was elected the first Christian king of Jerusalem. The First Crusade started in 1096 and was over in 1099, but the entire 11th century was essentially an age of pilgrimages and of church building.

There were three great objectives of pilgrimage: the Holy Land, where Christianity was born; Rome, the seat of the church; and Santiago de Compostela in northwestern Spain, the shrine of the Apostle St. James. There were many lesser shrines along the way and hostels for the pilgrims, many built by monks of the great Abbey of Cluny in Burgundy, the most powerful and richest monastic order of the period. The third church at Cluny, begun by the Abbot St. Hugh about 1089, was even larger than St. Peter's. The motivation for pilgrimages was, as Lord Clark points out, to ensure the future of one's soul through the intervention of the many saints whose relics were the objects of passionate devotion. No one knows how many tens of thousands went on pilgrimages during the Middle Ages, but they came from all walks of life, as we know from Chaucer's delightful descriptions in his famous *Canterbury Tales*. Probably more went to Santiago de Compostela than to the Holy Land, so distant and in the hands of the Moslems, and perhaps more than to Rome. In the 12th century a pious cleric even wrote a *Guide for the Pilgrims to Santiago*. In any event, along the various routes to Compostela many of the finest churches in the Romanesque style were built, including the cathedral of Santiago itself, all adorned with distinctive sculpture which often employed the flowing, curving line reminiscent of the dynamic interlace of Celtic art, seen, as Lord Clark indicates, at the Abbey of Moissac in the south of France.

Architecturally, the 11th century saw the rise of the Romanesque style, so-called because it was characterized by the use of the round arch common to the architecture of ancient Rome. Most Romanesque churches have barrel vaults—constructed as if one round arch were built after another to form a self-supporting stone covering. The finest examples are the Cluniac churches and those of the Pilgrimage Road: Santiago, St. Sernin at Toulouse, St. Martin at Tours, and St. Foy at Conques. One of the greatest is the cathedral of Durham, in the north of England, built by the Norman conquerors in their version of the Romanesque style, and begun in 1093. Fortress-like, it occupies the heights protected within a curve of the River Wear. Its lofty nave, massive columns and heavy towers are not only an expression of Norman strength but also look forward to the Gothic style of the next century—in the engineering of the vaulting, divided into bays marked by the great columns, and the flying buttresses which allow the nave's height.

The Benedictines of Cluny were the first of the powerful monastic

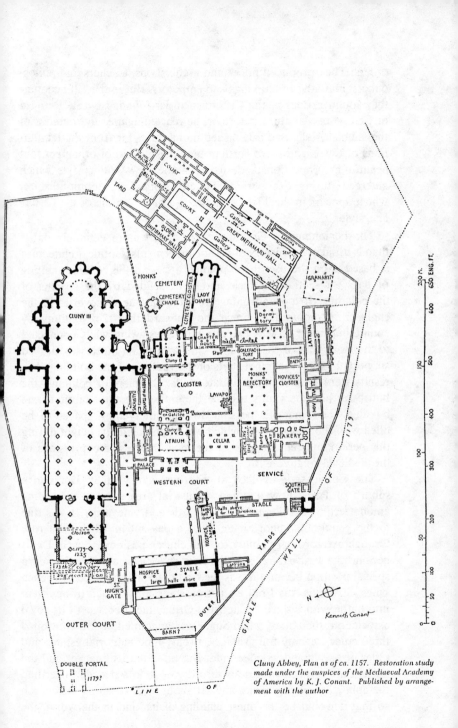

The following labels appear within the plan:

PRIORY BUILDINGS
YARD
YARD
COURT
COURT
Gallery
GREAT INFIRMARY HALL
OLDER INFIRMARY HALL
Gallery
Latrina
Stair

CLUNY III
MONKS' CEMETERY
CEMETERY CLOISTER
CEMETERY CHAPEL
LADY CHAPEL
[GRANARY?]
Dormitory
on upper level
LATRINA
CHAPTER HOUSE
CAMERA
Cluny II
Stair
CALEFAC-TORY
BATH
SACRISTY
CHAPEL of the ABBOT
Cluny I
en Galilee of
CLOISTER
LAVABO
MONKS' REFECTORY
NOVICES' CLOISTER
NOV.
SS.
TOILETTE
Court
Cluny I
ATRIUM
CELLAR
KITCHENS
Pilastered Court
BAKERY
PALACE
WESTERN COURT
SERVICE
SOUTH GATE
cloison
c. 1179-1225
13th century augmentation
Large hall
halls above for lay brethren
STABLE
HOSPICE
YARDS
WALL
OF
1179
ST. HUGH'S GATE
HOSPICE
large halls above
STABLE
Latrina
N
GIRDLE
OUTER
LINE OF
OUTER COURT
BARN?
Kenneth Conant
DOUBLE PORTAL
1179?

200 YT.
650 ENG. FT.
600
500
150
400
100
300
200
50
100
50
0

Cluny Abbey, Plan as of ca. 1157. Restoration study made under the auspices of the Mediaeval Academy of America by K. J. Conant. Published by arrangement with the author orders. They produced popes and archbishops, teachers and philosophers, and advisors to kings and emperors. But in the 12th century they found a rival in the Cistercian order founded by St. Bernard of Clairvaux. A natural reformer, he reacted against the richness of the Cluniac style, and established monasteries far from the temptations of towns and cities, austere buildings devoid of ornament, but beautifully proportioned, designed in the new Gothic style which emerged during this period. Tintern Abbey in Monmouthshire, which appears in the 11th program, is a fine example of the Cistercian style.

The beginnings of Gothic may be much more definitely dated than is usual in the history of artistic movements. Gothic architecture is based upon the use of the pointed arch and the cellular vaulting of bays, or sections of aisle and nave defined by the spacing of the columns. It took advantage of Romanesque discoveries in the engineering required to brace the outward thrust of vaulting by counterbalancing it with exterior buttresses—wing walls connected to the main wall of the building—and with flying buttresses, arched supports bracing the upper parts of the vaulting of the building. The results were virtually to eliminate walls: the piers or columns, the buttresses and the vaults became the entire structural fabric of the building. This made it possible for the intervening spaces to be filled with the stained glass which was approaching its height during this period and remains one of the most impressive expressions of the medieval creative spirit.

The Gothic style evolved at the royal abbey of St. Denis in a suburb of Paris—now a grimy, industrial area, but then standing among fertile, well-kept fields, orchards and vineyards. It was due to the genius of Abbot Suger, born a peasant in 1081, who rose through extraordinary ability to high church position, that St. Denis became the first example of the new style. The abbey occupied a special position because it was the traditional burial place of French kings. St. Denis was France's patron saint, and French troops went into battle with his red banner, the Oriflamme. Because of its royal association, the abbey, when Suger was appointed abbot, controlled three cities, seventy-four villages, twenty-nine manorial estates and miles of arable and wooded land. But he found its finances and the ancient abbey itself in serious disorder. Within a decade Suger had the abbey flourishing again, and set about reconstructing the church so that it would be the finest building of its kind in the world, the symbol of the monarchy and the sacred power, as defenders of the faith, of the French kings.

Work began in 1137 with a team of architects, designers, sculptors, goldsmiths and other craftsmen invited from all parts of France and beyond. The facade retains the Romanesque round arch, though its strong vertical emphasis is already Gothic in flavor. In the interior, in the choir, the new style appears full-fledged. Its tall columns—twelve in number to symbolize the Apostles—carry ribbed vaults; the walls are completely replaced by stained glass. The result is a composition whose soaring lightness completely expresses the new Gothic spirit.

The symbolism of the twelve columns came naturally to the medieval mind, especially to Suger's. He considered the light flooding through the stained glass windows as the Light of Truth, the spirit of Christ Himself. In the same way, he regarded the extraordinary richness of the furnishings of the Church—the altarpieces, reliquaries, crosses, church vessels and furniture, brilliant with color and precious metals and stones—as symbolic of the far greater richness of heaven. By means of the material, to paraphrase his own words, he sought to raise men's minds to the immaterial, from the worldly to the divine.

Though St. Denis is today but a shabby shadow of its former grandeur, the cathedral of Chartres (begun in 1145, burnt all except the facade, largely rebuilt by 1220), as Lord Clark points out, remains to show the glory of the Gothic toward which Suger aimed. According to medieval concept, the cathedral was the image of the world and each of its wonderfully diverse parts added up to a visual expression of that idea: the story of man's creation and fall, his redemption through Christ's sacrifice, the Old Testament prophets who had foretold what was to come, and the figures from the New Testament, their successors, the world of man and of nature, of earth and of heaven. The great age of cathedral building lasted little longer than a century. It started with Suger's St. Denis, dedicated in 1144, and its impetus was largely over by about 1250. Though countless churches continued to be built, few of the cathedrals were ever actually finished. Their completion was overtaken by time. The upper part of the north tower of Chartres, for instance, was not completed until after 1500, during the very years when Michelangelo's great dome for St. Peter's in Rome was being built, one of the crowning monuments of the Renaissance, the new era which was to follow.

All the great Gothic cathedrals were dedicated to the Virgin as Queen of Heaven, man's kindly intercessor against the finality of the Last Judgment. The cult of the Virgin was a strongly civilizing influence and was an aspect of what has been called the humanization of the saints which took place during the 13th century. It is also expressed in the life and works of St. Francis, who created the first crèche at Greccio, a little Italian town, in 1223, and in the legends of the lives of the saints incorporated in what became perhaps, after the Bible, the world's best seller, *The Golden Legend,* by Jacopo da Voragine, Archbishop of Genoa. In the arts the humanization appears in the representation of the Madonna as a charming girl-mother instead of the austere Queen of Heaven of the Romanesque period, of Byzantine art and of the earlier Gothic. It was yet another sign that the Age of Faith was waning, and another era was about to come.

Works of art as they appear in Program 2

Canterbury Cathedral, southeastern England (Kent). Norman church, 1071-77; choir or east end, 1174-85, erected by the French master-mason William of Sens. The Gothic style of the choir is influenced by that of the Ile-de-France, the area around Paris.

Montage of cathedrals and abbeys: Durham and Ely, England; Abbey of Aiguebelle and Chartres Cathedral, France; the Churches of Assisi, Italy; Abbey of Le Thoronet in France.

Ecclesia (the enthroned Madonna as symbol of the church), manuscript illumination. 12th century. Bayerische Bibliothek, Munich.

St. Augustine's Disciples, manuscript illumination from St. Augustine's *De Civitate Deo (The City of God).* Laurentian Library, Florence.

Building scenes, 12th century manuscript illuminations from *Claudis B IV,* British Museum, London; *The Book of St. Albans,* Trinity College, Dublin; and Mss. 27301 and 638, Pierpont Morgan Library, New York.

God the Architect of the Universe, manuscript illumination. 13th century. Austria National Library, Vienna.

Cluny Abbey, east-central France (Burgundy). 1089-1131. Founded in 910 by Benedictine order, Cluny became the greatest church in Europe under Hugh of Semur, abbot from 1049 to 1109. The Cluniac order spread quickly throughout Europe, founding 1,200 abbeys in France alone. The south transept is all that remains of the abbey church.

Dedication of Cluny Abbey, manuscript illumination. Bibliothèque Nationale, Paris.

Gloucester Candlestick. c. 1110. Gilt bronze, height 23″. Victoria and Albert Museum, London.

Abbey of Moissac, southern France. 12th century. The carvings with their sharp cutting, swirling drapery and twisting line are typical of Cluniac style. Sculptor of Moissac is known for his personal, angular manner. Sculpture shown here, c. 1115-36; tympanum relief, Christ of the Apocalypse with the 24 Elders and symbols of the Evangelists; porch relief and trumeau (mullion) of beasts; cloister capitals with monsters.

Cistercian Monasteries, 12th century. Abbey of Le Thoronet, southern France, founded c. 1160; monastery of Aiguebelle, southern France, founded 1137.

Scenes of Royal Crusades, manuscript illumination. 13th century. Shown here: King of France going on Crusade, British Museum, London (Royal 16G, VI); King with relic from Holy Land, Corpus Christi College Library, MS 16, Cambridge.

Conques, St. Foy at Conques, southwestern France. 11th century. Fine example of a Romanesque church. The miraculous reliquary made it a pilgrimage site.

Reliquary of St. Foy. Gold over wood, with jewels, cameos and crystal. Late tenth century. Treasury of Church of St. Foy, Conques.

Scenes of crusades, manuscript illuminations, 13th and 14th centuries, from Biblioteca del Seminario, Padua (MS 74); Bibliothèque Nationale, Paris (8572 Fr 4274); Pierpont Morgan Library, New York (M 638); British Museum, London (Royal 2 A XXII).

Elephants, Persian silk tapestry, Abbasid period. Second half of the tenth century. Louvre, Paris.

Initial C, manuscript illumination in Book of Jeremiah, from the Winchester Bible. c. 1160. Cathedral Library, Winchester.

Tree of Jesse, manuscript illumination from the Lambeth Bible. c. 1150. Lambeth Palace Library, London.

Vézelay, Abbey of, east-central France (Burgundy). Church of La Madeleine at Vézelay, begun about 1096; consecrated in 1104 and 1132. The style is Cluniac Romanesque. The nave ceiling is a vault separated by semicircular transverse arches. In 1146 St. Bernard of Clairvaux preached the Second Crusade to King Louis VII and a multitude of knights and faithful assembled on the hillside near Vézelay. Sculpture shown here, 1120-50: portico, or narthex, with three portals; central tympanum (c. 1130): *Christ Sending the Apostles to Preach throughout the World* (surrounding are scenes of legendary peoples at edge of world); capitals and decoration sculpture in nave.

Autun Cathedral, east-central France (Burgundy). 1090-1132. Romanesque. Gislebertus (active c. 1135) carried out all sculptural decoration of Autun Cathedral. Shown here: west tympanum with the *Last Judgment;* interior capitals, *Flight into Egypt, Three Wise Men* and *Suicide of Judas;* and *Eve,* a lintel segment now in Autun Museum.

St. Denis, Abbey of, near Paris. 1137-44, on site of earlier church. The abbey, dedicated to the patron saint of France, enjoyed the special patronage of the French kings. Shown here: the choir (1140-44), built by Abbot Suger, which marks the birth of the Gothic style; rose window, 13th century.

MASTER OF ST. GILES, *St. Giles Celebrating Mass in St. Denis.* 15th century. Panel, 24¼ x 18". National Gallery, London.

Vase in form of an eagle. c. 1140. Antique porphyry vase, 12th century additions of silver gilt. Height 17". From the Treasury St. Denis. Louvre, Paris.

Chartres Cathedral. Large, important cathedral southwest of Paris. Twelfth-century facade is all that remains after the fire of 1194; main body of cathedral built, 1195-1225. Spire of south tower, 12th century; of north tower, 16th century.

The facade (the earliest part of the cathedral) has 3 portals: on the jambs are pillar-like statues of Old Testament kings and queens; the tympanums have New Testament scenes glorifying Christ. The North Porch has figures from the Old Testament and the coming of the Messiah. Stained glass windows: the rose window and lancet of the west facade, 12th century; those elsewhere in the church, 13th century. Shown here: 12th-century rose window; scenes of the Creation *(God creating Adam and Eve, Tree of Knowledge)* from windows in the ambulatory; the famous window called *Notre Dame de la Belle Verrière,* including scenes of the death and funeral of the Virgin.

Virgin and Child, manuscript illumination from Cîteaux. 12th century. Bibliothèque Municipale, Dijon.

Ancient sculpture: shown here: 1) Maiden (Kore), No. 674. c. 540-

510, marble. Acropolis Museum, Athens; 2) Demeter from Knidos, fourth century B.C., marble, height 5′. British Museum, London; 3) Chatsworth *Apollo,* head from Salamis, Cyprus, c. 460 B.C., bronze, height 12½′. British Museum, London; 4) *Pericles,* mid-fifth century B.C., marble, height 20″. British Museum, London.

3. Romance and Reality

The High Gothic world, of chivalry and of courtly love, and the adoration of the Virgin; of the wordliness of the courts with their brilliant art and pageantry contrasted with the joyous asceticism of St. Francis; a period which saw the creation of Dante's great epic, the monumental painting of Giotto and the sculptures of Nicola and Giovanni Pisano, which epitomize the Gothic spirit.

"I am in the Gothic world, the world of chivalry, courtesy and romance; a world in which serious things were done with a sense of play—where even war and theology could become a sort of game; and when architecture reached a point of extravagance unequalled in history. After all the great unifying convictions of the 12th century, high Gothic art can look fantastic and luxurious—what Marxists call conspicuous waste. And yet these centuries produced some of the greatest spirits in the whole history of man, amongst them St. Francis of Assisi and Dante."

The 13th century saw the height of Gothic art and the continuation of the Crusades. The contacts of the rough, northern barons with the far more civilized Arab world made a profound impression on the development of European culture. The Crusaders saw not only the sophisticated life in the beautiful Greek-Christian city of Constantinople, but also that of the Moslems, whose houses and palaces (like the famous Alhambra in southern Spain) had plumbing and running water, a far cry from the draughty, smelly castles they were used to. They saw the richness of the intricately woven silks and damasks made in the East, many of which were to become church vestments in European cathedrals. They saw superbly wrought Arab ceramics and goldsmithwork, and developed an entirely new attitude toward life from that inherited from their barbarian ancestors. Furthermore, they found the Arabs at least as chivalrous and brave as themselves. The Frankish states in the Holy Land and the eastern end of the Mediterranean did not last long. In 1244 the Moslems recaptured Jerusalem. But the impact of Arab civilization was profound.

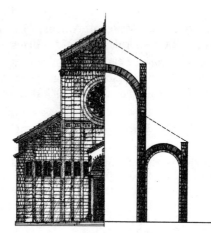

ROMANESQUE AND GOTHIC, *two major styles of architecture th* *evolved in Europe during the Middle Ages, were, in a sense, variations c* *the theme of the arched vault. In the 11th and 12th centuries, churc* *builders, following Roman models, rounded their arches and vaults (above* *and built massive walls to carry their weight. By the mid-12th century,* *was found that by pointing the arches, vaults could be built much high* *than before. Slender piers, propped by flying buttresses, supported t* *soaring Gothic vault (below). With walls freed for windows, churches b* *came virtual skeletons of stone illuminated by magnificent stained glas*

Arab scholars had translated into their own language many ancient Greek and Roman texts by great authors, especially in science and technology. In many cases these important legacies from the classical world were known in Europe only through translations from the Arabic; later, texts in classical languages began to be rediscovered, hidden in the libraries of monasteries.

Also, during the 13th century contact was made with the Far East. The Polo brothers of Venice and their more famous nephew, Marco, made their way to China, to return with both riches and tales of cities and a fabulous empire. Trade routes grew up to transmit the goods of the Far and Near East into Europe, first Constantinople and then Venice being the great mercantile emporiums. Cities became independent centers of trade, and commerce grew.

During the 13th century many of the great universities were founded: the charter of the University of Paris dates from 1200; the University of Naples was founded in 1224, by the Emperor Frederick II, the first in Europe with a royal charter. Frederick was of Norman and German ancestry, yet, living all his life in Sicily and Southern Italy, inherited a Mediterranean point of view. Redheaded, independent and devoid of superstition, he was guilty of what was considered a dreadful sin: tolerance. He welcomed Arabs, Jews, Greeks, even Mongols into his sophisticated court. Master of six languages, and an avid student of philosophy, classical literature, music and the arts, he wrote the definitive book on falconry. He gathered around himself the most gifted and imaginative personalities he could find, whatever their beliefs—scandalous behavior for the Holy Roman Emperor.

One of the great patrons of art and learning of all time, Frederick's enlightened attitudes, and his ambitions of a united Europe run by a professionally trained administration, instead of being constantly at war as one unruly baron fought another, were too far in advance of his times. The pope managed to unite his enemies against him, and he died in 1250, defeated, yet history has regarded him as the first modern man. With poetic justice, the power of the papacy declined with that of its chosen enemy, and a century of disruption followed.

Because it was based on a revival of classical culture and respect for the individual, the flowering of the arts which took place during Frederick's reign in the first half of the 13th century has been called the Proto-Renaissance, an anticipation by a century and a half of the movement which was to develop in Florence and usher in the modern world. Though his court and courtiers were dispersed at his death, most of the palaces and triumphal arches and monumental sculptures destroyed or severely damaged, his influence on the course of late medieval art and thought was profound.

In 1250 the sculptor Nicola d'Apulia (Apulia is a province in the southern tip of Italy), a refugee from the dead emperor's court, arrived in Pisa, and was thereafter known as Nicola Pisano. He brought with him his young son, Giovanni. These two men were among the greatest of medieval sculptors, their work full of reminiscences of the classical art they had seen in Frederick's court, but also full of the profound expressiveness of medieval faith. In their sense of true, bulky form, they were Giotto's counterparts. Like him, their art looks to the future—even to the achievements of Michelangelo—to the era which was to come, even while it embodies the highest ideals of the Middle Ages.

The 13th century saw the completion of the great work of St. Thomas Aquinas, the *Summa theologica,* in which he brought together into a unified whole the philosophical heritage of the classical past with the tenets of Christianity. It is a literary counterpart of the cathedral as the expression of the unity of the universe of which man is an essential and central part. The same spirit and search for unity underlies Dante's great poem. The sense of the unity of man and the universe is one of our major heritages from the Middle Ages.

From 1309-77, Avignon, in southern France, replaced Rome as the seat of the papacy during what was known as the Babylonian Captivity. During the 14th century the papacy split into factions, with rival popes vying for power. The Hundred Years War between France and England, and the plague—the infamous Black Death—ravaged Europe, and caused uprisings among the unfortunate peasantry in both France and England. It was a time of chivalry, as represented by the Black Prince, the warrior son of King Edward III of England. Yet change was in the air. It was the yeoman archers of England who beat the French knights at Crécy in 1346, and, about 1375, the plight of the peasantry was given its first literary expression in the poem called *The Vision of William Concerning Piers the Plowman* written by William Langland, an English country clergyman. Some ten years or so later, Geoffrey Chaucer began writing his incomparable *Canterbury Tales,* with its vivid array of characters from all walks of life, perhaps the first great work which may be truly called English literature.

During the 15th century, while the new era—the Renaissance—was being born in Florence and spreading throughout Italy, there was in the north the final flowering of Gothic art with the superb *Très Riches Heures* of the Duke of Berry by the Limbourg brothers (1413-16), the *Ghent Altarpiece* completed by Jan van Eyck in 1432 and the music and literature of the highly cultured court of Philip the Good (reigned 1419-76), Duke of Burgundy. Finally, at the very end of the century, the Unicorn Tapestries (now in The Cloisters, New York) were begun to celebrate the marriage of Anne of Brittany to Louis XII of France in 1499, and completed about 1514 when Anne's daughter married Francis I, the first Renaissance king of France.

In both France and England political stability was gradually won: in France, through the inspired leadership of Joan of Arc, and in England with the victory of Henry, Earl of Richmond, who became king in 1485, the first of the Tudors, whose greatest ruler was his granddaughter, Elizabeth. In 1469 the marriage of Ferdinand, king of Aragon, and Isabella, queen of Castille, ensured the unification of Spain, while in 1492 the Moslems were driven from Granada at the southern tip of Spain, making it one Christian kingdom. In the same year, Columbus made his first voyage to the New World. Vestiges of medievalism still remained in remoter parts of northern Europe, but a new era had arrived, a new chapter in history begun.

Works of art as they appear in Program 3

Cluny Museum, Paris. Formerly Palace of the Abbott of Cluny. Constructed 1485-1498 by Jacques d'Amboise.

The Lady with the Unicorn, French, c. 1490-1500. Tapestry in six panels. Cluny Museum, Paris. Shown here: *Taste, Smell, Hearing, Sight* and *A Mon Seul Desir.*

St. Modeste, jamb figure on north portal, 1225-35, Chartres Cathedral.

Sir Geoffrey Luttrell Bidding Farewell to his Wife and Daughter-in-Law. Manuscript illumination, British Museum, London.

Ivory boxes and mirror backs, showing courtly scenes. French, 14th century. Victoria and Albert Museum, London. Subjects shown:
  1) *Knights returning to the Castle of Lady with Unicorn in Lap;*
  2) *Knights and Ladies Riding;* 3) *Castle of Loire;* 4) *Knights Climb-*

ing Ladders; 5) *The Elopement* (Walker Art Gallery, Liverpool).

Virgin and Child, French, c. 1300, ivory, height 16⅛". Formerly in St. Chapelle; now Louvre, Paris.

Madonna and Child, French, c. 1300. Ivory statuette. Victoria and Albert Museum, London.

Two Maries at the Tomb, French, c. 1300. Ivory plaque. Victoria and Albert Museum, London.

Descent from the Cross, French, 14th century. Ivory statuette. Louvre, Paris.

MASTER OF RENÉ D'ANJOU, manuscript illuminations of René d'Anjou's *Le Livre du Coeur d'Amour Epris (Book of the Heart Captured by Love),* c. 1457. National Library, Vienna. (Cod. 2597) Shown: 1) *Outdoor scene, Coeur reads, Desir sleeps;* 2) *Night scene indoors, Love draws out Coeur's heart, gives it to Desir;* 3) *Boat scene, Coeur, Vig-Desir and Largesse with Fiance and Actente.*

THE LIMBOURG BROTHERS, manuscript illustration in *Très Riches Heures* of the Duke of Berry, 1413-16. Musée Condé, Chantilly. Contains 127 miniatures, 71 by the Limbourgs, the rest finished after their death. Shown: *12 calendar pages, January through December.* Note castles, occupations, festivities, and atmosphere.

Royal Gold Cup of the Kings of France and England. French, c. 1380, made for the Duke of Berry. Gold, enamels, pearls and precious stones, height 9¼". British Museum, London.

Reliquary of the Thorn. French, c. 1400. Gold, with jewels and enamel. British Museum, London.

St. Peter Receiving the Duke of Berry. Manuscript illumination, French, 15th century. Bibliothèque Nationale, Paris (MS Lat 919, fol. 96).

Birds, manuscript illumination from Pepysian Library, Magdalen College, Cambridge (Ms 1916), and Vatican Library (Vat. Lat. Ms 51.1r).

SASSETTA, St. Francis Altarpiece. 1437-44. Panel, scene shown: 1) *St. Francis Meets the Poor man;* 2) *St. Francis Gives Cloak to Poor Man;* 3) *Dream of St. Francis;* 4) *St. Francis and His Father;* 5) *St. Francis Receives Stigmata;* 6) *St. Francis and the Wolf of Gubbio.* National Gallery, London. 7) *St. Francis Moved to Poverty, Chastity, Obedience.* Musée Condé, Chantilly.

SASSETTA, *St. Francis in Glory.* 1437-44. Panel, 80¾x48". Berenson Collection, Florence.

GIOTTO, *Life of St. Francis.* Early 14th century. Frescoes, shown:

1) *St. Francis before Pope Honorius;* 2) *St. Francis Preaching.* Upper Church, San Francesco, Assisi.

CIMABUE, *Portrait (?) of St. Francis.* Late 12th century. Fresco. Lower Church, San Francesco, Assisi.

Upper and Lower Church of San Francesco, Assisi. 1228-53. Pilgrimage church built on a hill, hence, the upper and lower church. A good example of the Gothic style in Italy, it has frescoes by Cimabue and Giotto depicting St. Francis and incidents from the history of the Franciscan Order.

AMBROGIO LORENZETTI, *Good Government in the City.* c. 1338. Fresco. Palazzo Pubblico, Siena.

Palazzo Pubblico (Town Hall), Siena. 1289-1309 grandeur symbolizes the municipal life and enterprise of Siena in medieval days. It has a lofty watch tower and fortified facade.

Banking Scenes, manuscript illumination from *De Septem Vitiis.* Italian, late 14th century. British Museum, London. (MS. Add. 27695, fol. 8 octo).

QUENTIN MATSYS, *The Money-Changer and His Wife.* Flemish, 1514. Panel, 28x26¾". Louvre, Paris.

GIOTTO, *Life of the Virgin, Life of Christ.* 1305-6. Fresco. Arena Chapel, Padua. Shown: 1) *Joachim and the Shepherds;* 2) *Meeting at the Golden Gate;* 3) *Marriage of the Virgin;* 4) *Marriage at Cana;* 5) *Betrayal;* 6) *Lamentation;* 7) *Noli Me Tangere;* 8) *Last Judgment.*

CIMABUE, *Enthroned Madonna and Child.* Italian, c. 1280-90. Panel, 12'7½"x7'4". Uffizi Gallery, Florence.

DOMENICO DI MICHELINO, *Dante and the Heavenly City.* 1465. Fresco. Cathedral, Florence.

NICOLA PISANO, Marble pulpit. 1259-60. Baptistry, Pisa. Five reliefs of Life of Christ. Shown: *Last Judgment.*

GIOVANNI PISANO, Marble pulpit. 1302-10. Pisa Cathedral.

GIOVANNI PISANO, Marble pulpit. 1297-1300. San Andrea Fuorcivitas, Pistoia, Italy. Shown: *Massacre of the Innocents.*

4. Man—the Measure of All Things

The dramatic emergence of the modern world in fourteenth-century Florence, the city of the Medici—among the world's greatest patrons of art—of Donatello and Masaccio, Alberti and Brunelleschi, of Ghiberti and Botticelli, of Lorenzo the Magnificent; in the courts of Urbino and

Mantua; and in the proud Republic of Venice. It was a period when man felt that through the power of his rediscovered individuality he could accomplish wonders.

"The Pazzi Chapel, built in about 1430 by the great architect Brunelleschi, has rightly been described as the architecture of humanism. His friend and fellow architect, Leon Baptista Alberti, addressed man in these words: 'To you is given a body more graceful than other animals, to you power of apt and various movements, to you most sharp and delicate senses, to you wit, reason, memory like an immortal god.' Well, it is certainly incorrect to say that we are more graceful than other animals, and we don't feel much like immortal gods at the moment. But in 1400 the Florentines did. There is no better instance of how a burst of civilisation depends on confidence than the Florentine state of mind in the early fifteenth century."

The movement called the Renaissance—or rebirth—started in Florence in the early decades of the 15th century. It was based, again, on a shift of emphasis in man's idea of his relation to the world around him. Suddenly the present, not some distant, hoped-for future, took on a demanding immediacy. Following the almost forgotten ideals of the classical past, man rediscovered himself, not as a hapless pilgrim making his way through this world in search of the ultimate finality of heaven, but as an individual, unique in time, unique in personality, unique in potentiality, living vividly at the moment. In his endeavor to realize this rediscovery of himself through studying and emulating the achievements of Greece and Rome, Renaissance man created the modern era, with its emphasis on matters of this world and on a quest for personal realization with a sense of the swift passage of time.

The atmosphere of Florence was ripe for this change from the beginning of the 15th century. The early evidence of it was a series of works of art in sculpture and architecture. In 1401 the city announced a contest for the completion of the second set of bronze doors for the Florentine Baptistry (the first had been done in 1336). Brunelleschi, later to win fame as an architect, and Ghiberti, a goldsmith and sculptor, were principal contenders. The subject, the *Sacrifice of Isaac by Abraham,* was set as was the form the reliefs were to take—the medieval shaped panel used in the first set of doors. Both bronze trial reliefs are preserved. Brunelleschi's is full of drama, movement and realistic detail, skillfully composed. Ghiberti's panel substitutes Gothic grace for drama, yet has equal narrative clarity. The jury of artists chose Ghiberti's, and Brunelleschi, independent as always, turned primarily to architecture instead, though he never entirely gave up sculpture. And we know from historical evidence that he was a painter also, though none of his pictures has survived.

The project of the doors was so large and complex that it became a veritable art school for promising students who worked as Ghiberti's assistants. Among them was Donatello, the first great sculptor of the Renaissance. The doors were completed in 1424 and were so universally acclaimed that Ghiberti was commissioned to do the third pair, finally finished in 1452. In the latter, as Lord Clark points out, he used twelve large oblong panels in relief instead of the twenty-four smaller panels on the previous doors. Each panel has an extraordinary effect of depth achieved within what was actually a very shallow space. These were the doors that Michelangelo considered so beautiful as to be worthy to be the Gates of Paradise.

In 1406 Brunelleschi had already turned his attention to architecture in attempting what had been considered an insoluble problem, the construction of the vast dome of the Cathedral of Florence, started in 1298 by Arnolfo di Cambio, a Pisano follower who was a notable architect and sculptor. At Brunelleschi's advice, a gigantic octagonal drum was constructed around the opening to be crowned by the dome, thus letting light into the central area through eight enormous round windows, but also rendering the building of the dome yet more difficult. He knew exactly how he was going to do it, but, typically for a man of the Renaissance, he wished to be left free of committees and advisers to do it himself. For a period Ghiberti was appointed as co-engineer, but when the time came to start on the dome Brunelleschi merely bided his time until, in desperation, the committee left the matter entirely in his hands. He constructed the octagonal dome with an inner and an outer shell, entirely without centering—heavy wooden supports to hold up the structure until it became self-supporting—almost out of the question because of the dome's vast size. Using herringbone brickwork at the angles where the masonry supported itself, he built arches bridging the rising ribs which marked the corners of the octagon, and thus worked the masonry upward to a round opening topped with a lantern tower. Brunelleschi lived to see the dome itself done, but the tower was only finished in 1467, though to his own design. The result is one of the greatest domes in the world and an architectural and engineering feat which won him universal renown.

In the meantime, he designed the Foundling Hospital (1419-21), with its lovely arched loggia adorned with Luca della Robbia's charming reliefs in colored ceramic. The Pazzi Chapel, mentioned by Lord Clark, dates from 1429 to 1451. Because it is a purely architectural project, in its exterior it is somewhat tentative in design compared to the drama of the great dome. But in scale and subtlety of proportion in the interior, and in the use of the natural beauty of *pietra serena,* a fine greenish stone quarried near Florence, set off by plain white plaster walls, the only color supplied by della Robbia reliefs of the four Evangelists and the twelve roundels of the Apostles, it is a masterpiece of clarity and rational order, a direct expression of these qualities of Brunelleschi's mind, so typical of the Renaissance. The Old Sacristy of the Medici church of San Lorenzo, built by Brunelleschi from 1421 to 1429 with fine reliefs by Donatello, has a similar clarity of concept.

Brunelleschi's combination of art and science was typical of the Renaissance. Most Florentine artists were trained as craftsmen, many as goldsmiths, as is suggested by the minute but beautifully detailed work of Ghiberti. They were not specialists, but worked as architects, sculptors, painters, engineers, instrument-makers, etc. The sense of proportion apparent in all Brunelleschi's works, as in the works of so many other Renaissance artists, is the result of their interest in mathematics and in such systems of order as the science of perspective. The implications of this go far beyond the mere representation of depth on a flat surface. The development of perspective, first by Brunelleschi, then by Alberti, Piero della Francesca and Leonardo da Vinci, gave man an entirely different idea of himself in relation to space. It made possible urban planning on a grand scale, mapmaking and navigational charts. A modern space scientist has said that without this development in the Renaissance the whole modern space program would not have been possible. Perspective is, then, symbolic of another aspect of the profound philosophical change in man's idea of himself in relation to nature and the universe.

Alberti's famous book, *De Re Aedificatoria,* is the first great Renaissance treatise on architecture. He reestablished the Roman sense of scale and splendor which was later realized in designs by such architects as Michelangelo at St. Peter's. About 1450 he himself designed the Malatesta temple, a church commissioned by

Sigismondo Malatesta, the notorious tyrant of Rimini, and the Rucellai Palace in Florence (1446-51). Though of early Renaissance date, the latter already has High Renaissance grandeur.

Alberti was a contemporary of the first great Renaissance sculptor, Donatello, who was a friend of Brunelleschi and also of Cosimo de' Medici, the actual ruler of Florence and a great patron of the arts. Donatello's sculptures have the lean, athletic look one sees in Florentines even today. His female figures have an austere, classic beauty. He was capable of expressing the potentiality of power, as in the *Gattamelata,* his sculpture of a mounted general in Padua, whose quietly commanding figure controls with ease the immense charger on which he rides. Or his early *St. George,* whose tense vigilance looks forward to Michelangelo's *David,* so different from Donatello's graceful, though sinewy youth. Donatello also anticipates Michelangelo in his sense of the tragedy of life. His late, great bronze reliefs, such as those for the pulpits in San Lorenzo, show scenes of Christ's Passion in an almost impressionistic fashion, and with an agony and immediacy almost painfully moving. His sculpture in wood of St. Mary Magdalene, worn with ascetic discipline and purged by inner suffering, has immense and poignant power.

Luca della Robbia, another contemporary of Brunelleschi and Donatello, was trained first as a stone mason and then as a sculptor in stone. He was the first to use terra-cotta, baked clay which he glazed in color, primarily blue and white, as a medium of monumental sculpture. He started a dynasty of artists who continued for several generations in the same tradition, though none achieved his simplicity and authority.

The leading sculptor (who was, typically, also painter, goldsmith and engineer) of the generation following Donatello was Verrocchio, whose life-size bronze of Colleoni, a mercenary general, is one of the great equestrian statues, and also anticipates Michelangelo in its expression of power. He was the master to whom the young Leonardo da Vinci was apprenticed. The versatility of his practice was of the greatest value to the younger and far greater artist. Verrocchio's famous painting of *The Baptism of Christ* in the Uffizi contains two details by the young Leonardo, the heads of two attending angels, painted with the subtlety of modelling and expression which is typical of all his works.

Michelozzo—who was also a superb sculptor—designed the Medici Palace. One of the leading architects of the generation following

Brunelleschi and Alberti, he passed on their tradition to such leading High Renaissance architects as Bramante, first designer of the new St. Peter's, and to Michelangelo.

Masaccio, who disappeared from history while still a youth, shortly after completing his revolutionary frescoes in the Brancacci Chapel in the Church of the Carmine, had no immediate followers. Masaccio's figures, existing in a real space, have the bulk and weight of Giotto's; but, like the sculptures of Donatello, they have the feeling of the bodily structure beneath the clothing, while in Giotto figure and drapery seem of the same substance. This is but another example of man as "the measure of all things;" the nude human figure became, as in classical times, and as has remained true from the Renaissance until almost today, the most significant element of artistic expression.

Sandro Botticelli (1445-1510) was the favorite painter of the circle surrounding Lorenzo de' Medici, Lorenzo the Magnificent— patron, poet and lover of the arts and of learning—during the second half of the century. He inherited from his master, Fra Filippo Lippi (1406-69), the linear tendencies which he carried to poetic heights in such subjects as *The Birth of Venus* and *Spring,* inspired by the theories of Neo-Platonism, with its love of beauty, which attempted to fuse classical mythology with Christian faith. Neo-Platonism influenced all the arts associated with Lorenzo's circle, including his own poetry.

No artist of the period better carried on Masaccio's monumentality than Piero della Francesca (c. 1420-92), who made important contributions to the science of perspective. His fresco cycle in the church of San Francesco in Arezzo, a city south of Florence, which fill the apse with episodes recounting the story of the rediscovery of the true cross, are unmatched in their architectural sense of composition and heroic grendeur. Utterly static, they have a sense of silent timelessness unique in art.

Representing the opposing tendency, from the tradition established by Donatello, was Luca Signorelli (1445/50-1523), whose frescoes of the Last Judgment in the chapel of San Biagio in the cathedral of Orvieto, show the damned and the saved, in a series of dramatic episodes, full of often violent action in which the muscular nude becomes the artist's basic expressive means, an approach which Michelangelo was to carry to far greater heights.

There were strong connections between Florence and Padua,

to the north, near Venice. Giotto's Arena Chapel frescoes are there, and, more than a century later, Donatello did some of his finest sculptures there during a ten-year period. It is, then, no suprise that Andrea Mantegna (1431?-1506) of Padua emerged around the middle of the 15th century as a painter to be ranked with Masaccio and Piero della Francesca. Lork Clark discusses his work at Mantua, yet his frescoes, unfortunately destroyed by a bomb in 1944, in the Church of the Eremitani in Padua, showed at least equal mastery and yet greater power. The *St. James Led to Execution*, the saint's martyrdom, and that of St. Christopher, seen as if the viewer were standing at a lower level than the pictures (as is actually the fact in the church), are not merely a tour de force of perspective, but create a uniquely dramatic effect.

Mantegna was the brother-in-law of Giovanni Bellini (1430?-1516), whom Lord Clark characterizes as "the founder of Venetian painting." Bellini's pupil Giorgione was to give a new direction to the painting of the Venetian School, leading to the High Renaissance achievements of Titian and others, but whose work always retains an individual sense of mystery.

The connection between Italian painting and that of the late medieval North, already in transition to the new period, is a complex one. The realism of the van Eycks, which Lord Clark mentions, is certainly an important influence, being a continuation of the strain of realism which ran through later medieval art. But the introduction of the technique of oil painting, developed in the North, had perhaps an even more profound effect. The universal medium before the introduction of oil was egg tempera, the most permanent and stable type of painting yet invented. Capable of minute detail, tempera has a dry, matte surface, while oil has possibilities of transparency. Its surface seems not to intercept the viewer's vision, but to allow him to look through it into the picture space. What evolved from the introduction of oil as a medium made possible the extreme richness of color and tone, the transparency of shadow and the rendering of light and atmosphere which characterize Western painting from the High Renaissance on.

Works of art as they appear in Program 4

ARNOLFO DI CAMBIO, Palazzo Vecchio (Palace of the Signoria),

Florence. 13th century, tower finished in the 14th century. Florentine town hall.

BENEDETTO DA MAIANO, the Strozzi Palace, Florence. Begun 1490.

LUCA DELLA ROBBIA, *Evangelists*. 1442-51. Terra-cotta plaques in Pazzi Chapel, Florence.

FILIPPO BRUNELLESCHI, Pazzi Chapel. Begun 1430. In cloister of Santa Croce, Florence.

Brancacci Chapel, Church of the Carmine, Florence.

MASACCIO, *St. Peter Healing with His Shadow*. 1425. Fresco. Brancacci Chapel, Florence.

MASACCIO, *St. Peter Distributing Alms*. 1425. Fresco. Brancacci Chapel, Florence.

MASACCIO, *St. Peter Enthroned* (completed by Filippino Lippi). 1481-83. Fresco. Brancacci Chapel, 1425.

MASACCIO, *The Tribute Money*. 1425. Fresco. Brancacci Chapel, Florence.

BERNARDO ROSSELLINO, Tomb of Leonardo Bruni. 1444. Marble. Santa Croce, Florence.

Petrarch in His Study, from *De viris Illustribus (Concerning Famous Men).* c. 1380. Manuscript illumination. Landesbibliothek, Darmstadt (Codex 101).

Cino da Pistoia Teaching the Scholars, relief from the Tomb of Cino. c. 1337. Marble. Cathedral, Pistoia.

VITTORE CARPACCIO, *St. Jerome in His Study* (detail of tools), 1502-07 Oil on canvas. Scuola di San Giorgio degli Schiavoni, Venice.

ANTONELLO DA MESSINA, *St. Jerome in His Study*. c. 1475. Panel, 18x14⅛″. National Gallery, London.

MICHELOZZO, Library of San Marco, Florence. c. 1440.

BRUNELLESCO. Cloisters, Santa Croce, c. 1430. Florence.

Baptistry, Santa Maria della Fiore, Florence.

GIULIANO DA SANGALLO, Santa Maria delle Carceri. Begun 1484. Prato.

LEONARDO DA VINCI, *Study of Human Proportions after Vitruvius*. Pen and ink, 13½x9¾″. Accademia, Venice.

LORENZO GHIBERTI, East doors of Baptistry (called Gates of Paradise). 1425-52. Gilded bronze. Florence. Shown: 1) *Creation of Adam;* 2) *Jacob and Esau;* 3) *Story of Joseph.*

DONATELLO, reliefs from High Altar. Bronze with gold and silver, 22½x48½″. Shown: *St. Anthony Heals the Young Man's Foot;*

Miracle of the Talking Ass. St. Antonio, Padua.

FRANCESCO DI GIORGIO (attrib.), *Perspective of a Town.* Drawing, pen and ink. Galerie, Dresden.

PIERO DELLA FRANCESCA (?), *View of Ideal Town.* Late 15th century. Panel. Walters Art Gallery, Baltimore.

PIERO DELLA FRANCESCA (?), *View of Ideal City.* Late 15th century. Panel. Museo Nazionale delle Marche, Palazzo Ducale, Urbino.

Month of Mercury, (view of Florentine street scene). 15th century. Engraving.

MICHELANGELO BUONAROTTI, *Pitti Madonna.* Marble, diameter 33″. Bargello (Museo Nazionale), Florence.

DONATELLO, *David and Goliath.* c. 1430-32. Bronze, height 62¼″. Bargello (Museo Nazionale), Florence.

Bargello, (formerly Palazzo del Podesta, now Museo Nazionale). Late 13th, early 14th centuries. Florence.

ANDREA DA FIRENZE, *Church Militant and Triumphant.* c. 1365. Fresco. Spanish Chapel, Santa Maria Novella, Florence.

DONATELLO (?), *Portrait of Niccolo da Uzzano.* c. 1440. Painted terra-cotta. Bargello(Museo Nazionale), Florence.

LEON BATTISTA ALBERTI, *Self-Portrait.* Bronze Medal. Kress Collection, National Gallery of Art, Washington, D.C.

DONATELLO, *Equestrian Statue of Gattamelata.* 1445-50. Bronze, height of group, about 11′. Piazza del Santo, Padua.

JAN VAN EYCK, *Portrait of the Artist's Wife.* 1439. Panel, 12⅝x10¼″. Musée des Beaux-Arts, Bruges.

JAN VAN EYCK, *Portrait of Cardinal Niccolò Albergati.* Panel, 13⅜x10⅝″. Kunsthistorisches Museum, Vienna.

JAN VAN EYCK, *Portrait of Giovanni Arnolfini.* c. 1435. Panel, 11⅜x8″. Gemäldegalerie, Berlin-Dahlem.

JAN VAN EYCK, *Man with a Pink.* Panel, 15¾x12⅛″. Gemäldegalerie, Berlin-Dahlem.

JAN VAN EYCK, *Man with the Red Turban.* c. 1434. Panel. National Gallery, London.

JAN VAN EYCK, *Giovanni Arnolfini and Wife.* 1434. Panel, 32¼x23½″. National Gallery, London.

ANTONIO ROSSELLINO, *Portrait of Giovanni Chellini.* 1456. Marble, height 20′. Victoria and Albert Museum, London.

BENEDETTO DA MAIANO, *Portrait of Pietro Mellini.* 1474. Marble, height 27′. Bargello (Museo Nazionale), Florence.

Death-Mask of Lorenzo de' Medici. 1492. Medici-Riccardi Palace,

Florence.

Lorenzo de' Medici in the Streets of Florence, woodcut and frontispiece to his *Canzone a Ballo.* c. 1460-80.

DOMENICO GHIRLANDAIO, portraits of Lorenzo de' Medici and others in *Conforma della Regola (Institution of the Franciscan rule)* from *Life of Saint Francis.* 1484. Fresco. Sassetti Chapel, Santa Trinita, Florence.

SANDRO BOTTICELLI, *Spring.* c. 1477-78. Panel, 6'8"x10'4". Uffizi Gallery, Florence.

SANDRO BOTTICELLI, *The Birth of Venus.* c. 1480. Canvas, 5'9"x9'2". Uffizi Gallery, Florence.

SANDRO BOTTICELLI, *Madonna of the Pomegranate.* 1487. Panel, diameter 56¼". Uffizi Gallery, Florence.

PIERO DELLA FRANCESCA, *Portrait of Federigo Montefeltro.* 1465. Panel, 18½x13". Uffizi Gallery, Florence.

Palace of Urbino. c. 1444-82. Built for Federigo Montefeltro, the Palace began as a fortress. Laurana took over the work around 1465. The palace has unique, delicate decorative style which Kenneth Clark traces to Piero della Francesca. Shown are courtyards, stairs, open window with Della Robbia relief beyond, Duchess's room, mantels decorated with sphinxes and cupids, *studiolo* (Duke's study) with illusionistic wood inlay.

PIERO DELLA FRANCESCA, *Flagellation of Christ.* c. 1450. Panel, 23¼x32". Ducal Palace (Galleria Nazionale della Marche), Urbino.

RAPHAEL, *Youthful Self-Portrait* (about age 13). c. 1495. Drawing. Ashmolean Museum, Oxford.

PINTURICCHIO, *Life of Aeneas Sylvius Piccolomini.* 1503-08. Fresco. Library, Siena. Shown are *Embassy of James I of Scotland to Council of Basel* and *Crowning of the Poet.*

RAPHAEL, *Portrait of Baldassare Castiglione.* c. 1515. Canvas, 32¼x26½". Louvre, Paris.

ANDREA MANTEGNA, frescoes in Camera degli Sposi, Ducal Palace, Mantua. 1471-74. Shown: ceiling, heads looking down; and walls, the Gonzaga family and the arrival of Cardinal Francesco Gonzaga.

PIERO DELLA FRANCESCA, *Sigismondo Malatesta Kneeling Before His Patron Saint.* 1451. Fresco (now transferred to canvas). San Francesco, Rimini.

PIERO DELLA FRANCESCA, *Madonna and Child, Saints, Angels and Federigo Montefeltro (Madonna of the Egg).* c. 1475. Panel, 8'1¾"x 5'7". Brera Gallery, Milan.

JUSTUS VON GHENT, *Federigo Montefeltro Reading.* c. 1475. Galleria Nazionale della Marche, Urbino.

JAN and HUBERT VAN EYCK, Ghent Altarpiece. Completed 1432. Panel. Shown: *Adoration of the Lamb* and landscapes in side panels. Church of St. Bavo, Ghent.

GIOVANNI BELLINI, *Agony in the Garden,* c. 1480. Panel, 35x50″. National Gallery, London.

GIORGIONE, *Fête Chàmpetre.* c. 1510. Canvas, 43¼x54¼″. Louvre, Paris.

GIORGIONE, *The Tempest.* c. 1505. Canvas, 30¾x28⅜″. Accademia, Venice.

GIORGIONE (?). *Portrait of an Old Woman (Col Tempo).* c. 1510. 27⅛x23⅝″. Accademia, Venice.

5. The Hero As Artist

The High Renaissance flowered in Rome under the great humanist pope, Julius II, patron of Michelangelo—architect, painter, sculptor and poet— of Raphael, of Bramante and his grand concept for new St. Peter's, and of Leonardo da Vinci, whose vision looked beyond his period and on into worlds yet to come.

"Pope Julius II was not only ambitious for the Catholic Church; he was ambitious for Julius II; and in his new temple he planned to erect the greatest tomb of any ruler since the time of Hadrian. It was a staggering example of superbia—what we call megalomania; and Michelangelo at that time was not without the same characteristic. I need not go into the question of why the tomb was never built. All that matters is that some of the figures made for it survive, and they add something new to the European spirit—something that neither antiquity nor the great civilisations of India and China had ever dreamed of."

The comparatively short period known as the High Renaissance was not only a period in itself, but a moment of transition during which a few very great personalities produced some of the outstanding works of the Western World. It was limited almost entirely to Italy, with Rome and Venice as its primary centers. In the meantime, the principles and attitudes of the Renaissance style and spirit were gradually making themselves felt elsewhere, in Germany with Albrecht Dürer; in Central Europe, where Matthias Corvinus, the humanist King of Hungary, commissioned works from the greatest of Italian Renaissance artists; in France, where late medieval painting merged with the new spirit in the remarkable works of such outstanding painters as Jean Fouquet (c. 1420-81) and the anonymous Master of Moulins (15th-16th centuries).

The leading High Renaissance masters were, in order of age, Bramante (1444-1514), designer of new St. Peter's; Leonardo da Vinci (1452-1519); Albrecht Dürer (1471-1528) of Nuremberg, whose early visits to Italy led to a style which, while retaining certain late Gothic elements, became increasingly Renaissance though always northern in spirit; Michelangelo (1475-1564); Giorgione (1475-1510); Raphael (1483-1520); and Titian (1488/90-1576). All were Italians except Dürer. Leonardo and Michelangelo were Florentines by origin and training. Bramante, a north Italian, was much influenced by Leonardo while both were at the court of the Duke of Milan before Bramante went to Rome. Giorgione, born in the little north Italian town of Castelfranco, was a member of the Venetian school, of which Titian was the greatest master. Since Lord Clark studies Dürer in some detail in the 6th program, *Protest and Communication,* his work will be considered there.

The death of Lorenzo the Magnificent in 1492 coincided with Columbus's first voyage, and the election of the notorious Rodrigo Borgia as Pope Alexander VI. All three events heralded a new era: Lorenzo's death resulted in the shift in leadership in the arts from Florence to Rome; Columbus's voyage gave a strong impetus to the pursuit of exploration and discovery which changed men's concept of the world; and the election of Alexander brought about a lowering of respect for the papacy which had long-lasting reactions.

On Alexander's death in 1503—appropriately in suspicious circumstances—Julius II, a man of heroic spirit and determination, succeeded him. Julius was the great patron of Michelangelo, Raphael, Bramante and the many other painters, sculptors and architects who made Rome during his reign a vital artistic center. Julius was pope for only ten years, being succeeded in 1513 by Cardinal Giovanni de' Medici, son of Lorenzo the Magnificent, as Leo X. Yet few decades in history were as creatively productive as those of Julius's pontificate.

Leo was a man of a different stamp. Cultured, a connoisseur of the arts—as was natural for the son of such a father—he was an avid collector as well as a patron. But he entirely lacked Julius's warrior-like spirit; the ease and luxury of his court, and his indiscriminate sale of indulgences—remission of punishment for sins—to finance his artistic aims, helped speed the spirit of reform, growing for some time within the church, to produce the open revolt led by Martin Luther and others, called the Reformation, which irrevocably split the church in a division which has lasted to our own day.

Florentine artists of the Renaissance considered themselves craftsmen rather than artists in the modern sense. Neo-Platonic theory, however, cultivated in the circle surrounding Lorenzo the Magnificent in the later years of the 15th century, borrowed the Platonic idea of the artist as a genius, his work the result of divine inspiration, sharing the capacity of creation with God. Such ideas would have been unacceptable, indeed highly suspect, to an earlier artist such as Donatello, but in the 16th century the artist as genius became an accepted concept. This inspired High Renaissance artists to the greatest achievements, but it also led to their attempting works of such vast grandeur as almost to defy mere human effort for their realization. Therefore the whole scale of art, and the idea of the artist's relation to society, changed during the comparatively brief period of the High Renaissance, whose greatest works were produced only between about 1490 and 1525. Michelangelo and Titian long outlived the latter date, and both continued vigorously to produce until their last hours of life. Their later works were artistically ever grander and more impressive, yet, as the times changed, they became almost anachronistic in terms of contemporary style, though timeless in the judgment of history.

When Julius made the weighty decision to demolish the most revered church in Christendom, save only for that in Jerusalem, and replace it with a building of even greater size and grandeur, he was breaking dramatically with the past, but committing his successors for a century and more to a formidable and extremely expensive undertaking. True, the ancient Constantinian basilica had been sorely neglected, but its historic and religious connotations were so strong that there would have been every reason to repair and restore it to its original dignity, thus emphasizing the continuity of the church. Julius's decision represented a new spirit, an updating of the church to give it an even grander and more monumental authority. In such extraordinary individuals as Bramante, Michelangelo and Raphael he found men who could share and give superb expression to his aspirations.

Michelangelo was the son of minor Florentine nobility. The Buonarroti family has been recorded in the archives of the city as respectable and rather undistinguished. His father was an unimaginative, stodgy minor official who served as local governor of several small towns in Florentine territory, in one of which Michelangelo was born. He was one of several children, all the rest completely ordinary individuals. However one accounts for genius, he was one, and, like his older contemporary, Leonardo, it was apparent from the beginning. He studied briefly with Domenico Ghirlandaio (1449-94), a painter who produced some excellent frescoes and panel paintings, including portraits, marked by clear observation and competence rather than inspired imagination. Michelangelo's precocious talent was soon discovered by Lorenzo de' Medici, who gave him the run of the Medici collections and encouraged his study with the artist in charge of them, Bertoldo di Giovanni (1420?-91), a follower of Donatello. With Bertoldo he learned to sculpture in stone, and found his natural expression, because all his works— paintings and architecture as well—are essentially sculptural in concept. For him, three-dimensional form, the human form, was the basic medium of creative expression. And no one, except perhaps Rembrandt in his mature paintings, ever used it as powerfully to realize man's highest hopes and aspirations, and to express both the triumph and the tragedy of the human condition.

Michelangelo's last works were two sculptured groups depicting the removal of Christ's body from the Cross and Mary's mourning over her Son. In the first of these, Joseph of Arimathea, who gave his own tomb for Christ's burial, is a tragic self-portrait. This sense of a disintegration of faith, of the world's falling to pieces, shown also, as Lord Clark points out, by Leonardo's late drawings, haunted Michelangelo during his last years. It is the theme of some of his most moving poetry—he was incomparably the greatest Italian poet of his period—and it is recorded that he was at work on a sculpture on the same theme, never finished, within hours before his death at the age of almost ninety.

His sculptures for the Medici Chapel in San Lorenzo in Florence, with a Madonna whose expression, as she nurses her Son, shows her awareness of what He was to suffer, with the brooding figures of the two minor Medici princes, and the incomparable pairs of half-reclining figures of Dawn and Evening, Night and Day show what Michelangelo's contemporaries called his *terribilità,* his awesome— almost frightening—power to express tragic grandeur.

Raphael, son of the court painter of the Duke of Urbino, studied under the Umbrian artist, Perugino (c. 1450-1523), whose figures are graceful, compositions well-organized, and soft Umbrian landscape backgrounds are poetic in feeling. Raphael, too, was precocious. Vigorous, hard-working, even-tempered, and with an attractive personality far different from Michelangelo's individualistic and often irascible temperament, Raphael undertook countless commissions, aided by a small army of assistants whom he expertly organized. He was a gifted architect as well as painter, and his death at the age of thirty-seven undoubtedly deprived the world of a long series of remarkable achievements.

About Giorgione comparatively little is known. Before his death at 35 he had become established in Venice, and had produced large mural commissions, since destroyed, and a series of pictures whose sensuous poetry achieved through luminous color, enriched by light and shade, set the mood for subsequent Venetian painting. Several of his outstanding pictures, like the *Tempest* mentioned by Lord Clark, are similarly enigmatic and seem to deal rather with mood than with subject in the usual sense, and thus anticipate the Romantic movement of the later 18th and 19th centuries.

There is rarely anything enigmatic about Titian's canvasses. Untroubled, unlike Michelangelo, with matters of faith and conscience, his opulent paintings of nude Venuses are less goddesses than courtesans, his religious pictures marvelously orchestrated compositions with an oriental richness of color. His portraits are masterful, and his self-portrait as an old man shows him, full of vigor and assurance, a Venetian grandee. His latest works show a freedom of brushwork and interplay of color which suggest the painting of the Impressionists of four centuries later.

Though Leonardo da Vinci was the first of the great High Renaissance artists except for Bramante, Lord Clark appropriately considers him last among the heroes as artists because in the extraordinary breadth of his interests and the projection of his vision he excelled all the rest.

Leonardo was the illegitimate son of a young notary of respectable family, long established in the hill town of Vinci, west of Florence, and a country girl named Caterina. He first lived with his mother on a farm near Vinci, and there developed his love of nature and extraordinary keenness of observation. When his father married, the young wife took him into her home, and when the family moved to Florence, Leonardo was apprenticed to the leading artist of the time, Verrocchio. In Verrocchio's shop he learned all the diverse skills—from architecture to instrument-making, illumination to fresco painting, bronze-casting and marble cutting to color-grinding—which were expected of the Florentine artist of the period. He studied with the best mathematician of the age, Benedetto d'Abbaco, and Greek and Latin with humanist scholars of the Medici court, for Lorenzo was, as usual, quick to recognize his genius. During his stay later at the court of the Duke of Milan, he was in charge of the canal system of Lombardy, was a military engineer, court painter, composer and designer of masques and pageants, and studied anatomy. Though he seemed the complete courtier, he actually was working on a life-long search for truth. "Art and science are but two means to the same end," he wrote in his notebooks, "knowledge, the aim of all good men."

Without question the most versatile of artists who has ever lived, Leonardo brought all his artistic insights and training to a pursuit of knowledge, and thus is unique in history. In the process, he left a few masterpieces of painting, and the incredibly varied record of his notebooks. The recent discovery of the Madrid Manuscripts, in which the original order of several of the notebooks has been largely undisturbed, disproves the old theory that his life was aimless, his genius wasted. They contain, virtually ready for the publisher, two of the many treatises in which he intended to codify the results of his life-long search. As an example of the creative mind moving freely across the man-made boundaries which are supposed to divide the areas of activity of artists and scholars, he anticipates the man of the age of space, for whom the arts and the sciences are equal avenues for creative endeavor, and for whom, also, knowledge of man, of nature and of the forces of life itself, is the ultimate aim.

The brief moment of the High Renaissance was succeeded by what has been called Mannerism, in part a reaction to the clarity and logic of the Renaissance (a reaction suggested in Giorgione), and a transitional phase leading into the Baroque of the late 16th and 17th centuries. It is exemplified in architecture as well as in painting and sculpture. Bartolommeo Ammanati (1511-92) showed it in his designs for the courtyard and the enlarging of the Pitti Palace in Florence. Giovanni Bologna (1529-1608), a Fleming who became a completely Italian sculptor, showed it in his famous bronze *Mercury*. It appears in the works of the goldsmith and sculptor, Benvenuto Cellini (1500-71), such as his large *Nymph of Fontainebleau* and his famous salt cellar, done for Francis I. In painting it appears in the work of Jacopo Robusti, better known as Tintoretto (1518/19-94) of Venice, and the even more famous El Greco (1541-1614), born in Crete and trained in Venice, who found his spiritual home in Spain.

The movement is called Mannerism because many artists of the next generation, including literary figures, fastened upon certain aspects of style of the great masters of the High Renaissance, and gave them special emphasis. In its often illogical use of space, in enigmatic pose, suavity and elongation of form, and sometimes esoteric choice of subject, it anticipates certain aspects of the more powerful and positive Baroque style which was to follow.

Works of art as they appear in Program 5

Equestrian statue of Marcus Aurelius. Ancient bronze statue of Roman Emperor Marcus Aurelius (121-180) on horseback. Served as inspiration for Renaissance equestrian monuments. Campidoglio, Rome.

Campidoglio. The civic square at the top of the Capitoline Hill in Rome reshaped by Michelangelo in the 16th century. It was the most ambitious architectural commission and the most imposing civic center of the era. Palaces on three sides face a trapezoidal piazza, the focal point of which is the ancient equestrian bronze of Marcus Aurelius, placed on a base designed by Michelangelo.

Vatican. Collection of papal palaces adjacent to St. Peter's in the Vatican City. It includes the Vatican Museum and Library, the Sistine Chapel, the Loggias and the Stanzas (rooms decorated by Raphael and other artists), courtyards and gardens.

Belvedere. As designed by Bramante for Julius II, the Courtyard of the Belvedere in the Vatican was a huge court complex leading up a hill to a small summer house (Belvedere) overlooking Rome. The original plan has been much altered by subsequent building. The huge Pine Cone Niche is at one end of the original Belvedere.

Pine Cone. Heroic-sized bronze sculpture, probably once the finial of the tomb of the Roman Emperor Hadrian. Christians of the Middle Ages believed it to have come from the ancient Hippodrome where many Christian martyrs were killed; before it was placed in its niche in the Vatican, it stood in old St. Peter's.

The Roman Forum. The original market place or public square of the ancient city of Rome extending from the Senate building to the Temple of Venus and Roma. The Forum's monumental architecture was copied throughout the Roman Empire; its ruins can be seen in Rome today.

Piazza of St. Peter's. Huge entrance area (650 ft. wide) in front of the Cathedral of St. Peter, surrounded by colonnades and statues designed by the architect Bernini in the 17th century. It is considered the greatest of all approaches to the greatest of all churches in the Christian world. For centuries huge crowds have gathered here to be blessed by the Pope.

A fifteenth-century pope (probably Nicholas V) at window of the Vatican. Contemporary engraving.

MELOZZO DA FORLI, *Sixtus IV and His Scholars.* 1477. Fresco. Vatican Museum, Rome. Shows Pope Sixtus IV with the humanist and scholar Platina. In the background is Cardinal Giuliano della Rovere, later Pope Julius II.

RAPHAEL, *The Expulsion of Heliodorus,* detail showing Pope Julius II being carried in a chair. 1511-14. Fresco. Stanza d'Eliodoro, Vatican.

RAPHAEL (?), *Portrait of Julius II.* Uffizi Gallery, Florence.

Old St. Peter's. Fourth-century basilica built by the Emperor Constantine over what was believed to be the tomb of St. Peter. Despite repairs it was greatly decayed by the beginning of the 16th century when Julius II decided to tear it down. The demolition of the old basilica and beginnings of the new St. Peter's were recorded in 16th-century drawings by Maerten van Heemskerck (1498-1574). Shown here: 1) *Interior of Old St. Peter's,* fresco, Chiesa di San Martino ai Monti, Rome; 2) Heemskerck, *Loggia and Old St. Peter's,* drawing, British Museum, London; 3) Engraving, *Old St. Peter's.*

Apollo Belvedere. Roman marble copy, probably of an original Greek statue of the late fourth (or first) century B.C. During the 18th and 19th centuries, it was thought to be the perfect example of classic beauty. Height, 7'4". Vatican Museum, Rome.

BENOZZO GOZZOLI, *Rape of Helen.* c. 1450. Panel, irregular octagon, 20x24". National Gallery, London.

APOLLONIO DI GIOVANNI (?), *Death of Julius Caesar.* c. 1450. (Detail from *Scenes of the Life of Julius Caesar*). 15½x53¼" (whole). Ashmolean Museum, Oxford.

ANDREA MANTEGNA, *Triumph of Caesar.* c. 1486-97. Painted for the Gonzaga family, Mantua. Nine paintings on canvas which present a turbulent succession of musicians, bearers and the triumphant chariot of Caesar. The Royal Collection, Hampton Court.

DONATELLO, *Marzocco, or Lion of Florence*. Shown is a bronze copy in Piazza della Signoria; the marble original is in the Bargello Museum, Florence.

DONATELLO, *Judith and Holofernes*. Bronze, height 7'8⅞". c. 1460. Piazza della Signoria, Florence.

MICHELANGELO, *David*. 1501-4. Marble, height 13'5". Heroic in proportion and concept; considered one of the greatest works of Western Art. Original in Accademia, Florence; copy in Piazza della Signoria, Florence.

ANDREA DEL VERROCCHIO, *David*. Before 1476. Bronze, height 49½". Bargello Museum, Florence.

MICHELANGELO, *St. Proculus*. c. 1495. Marble statue, shrine of St. Dominic, San Domenico, Bologna.

MICHELANGELO, *Battle of the Lapiths and the Centaurs*. Marble relief, 33⅛x35⅜". Casa Buonarroti, Florence.

MICHELANGELO, *Bacchus*. c. 1496. Marble, height 6'. Bargello Museum, Florence.

MICHELANGELO, *Tomb of Julius II*. Michelangelo made several designs for the tomb over the years 1505-45, but its building was hampered by quarrels with the Pope and his heirs. It is noted more for the figures that Michelangelo carved for it, than for the completed whole that is in San Pietro in Vincoli, Rome, Julius II's titular church. Shown are the following figures intended for the tomb: *Dying Slave*. c. 1513-16, marble, 7'6⅛", Louvre, Paris. *Rebellious Slave,* c. 1513-16, marble, 7', Louvre, Paris. *Unfinished Slave,* also known as the *Awakening Captive,* marble, Accademia, Florence.

Sistine Chapel. Built for Sixtus IV as a private chapel in the Vatican, 1473-81, it is noted more for its interior frescoes than its architecture. The walls were painted by many important 15th-century painters, including Botticelli and Perugino; the magnificent ceiling frescoes of Michelangelo dominate the interior. Papal elections by the College of Cardinals are held in the Sistine Chapel.

MICHELANGELO, Sistine Ceiling. Series of frescoes commissioned for the ceiling of the Sistine Chapel by Pope Julius II and completed in only four years (1508-12). In the central area are nine scenes from *Genesis* surrounded by figures of nude youths called Athletes. Below are the Prophets and Sibyls and still lower, the Ancestors of Christ. Shown here: details from the *Flood,* the *Temptation of Adam and*

Eve, their *Expulsion from the Garden of Eden,* nude *Athletes,* the *Prophets Ezekiel* and *Jeremiah,* the *Drunkenness of Noah, God Dividing Light and Darkness,* the *Creation of Adam, God Dividing the Water,* and *God Creating the Sun and Moon.*

RAPHAEL, *Marriage of the Virgin.* 1504. Panel, 5′6⅞″x3′10½″. Brera, Milan.

Stanzas of Raphael. Rooms in the Vatican Palace decorated by Raphael and his assistants for Popes Julius II and Leo X, 1509-14. Includes the Stanza della Segnatura (1509-12) and the Stanza d'Eliodoro (1511-14). Shown here: 1) the *Disputà* (Divine Reason), 2) the *School of Athens* (Human Reason) and 3) *Parnassus* (Poetic Inspiration), all from the Stanza della Segnatura; portrait of Julius II, a detail from the *Mass of Bolsena,* in the Stanza d'Eliodoro.

RAPHAEL, *Drawings for the Disputà.* Stanza della Segnatura, Vatican. One is now in the British Museum; the other in the Städelsches Kunstinstitut, Frankfurt.

RAPHAEL, *Pope Leo X with Cardinals Giulio de' Medici and Luigi de' Rossi.* c. 1518. Panel, 5′⅝″x3′10⅞″. Uffizi Gallery, Florence.

Loggias of Raphael. Gallery in three parts overlooking the Court of St. Damaso in the Vatican. Decorated by Raphael's pupils after his own designs. Includes fifty-two scenes from Old and New Testaments.

RAPHAEL. Cartoons for tapestries which were to be hung in the Sistine Chapel, 1515-6. Shown are the *Miracle of the Loaves and Fishes* and *Feed My Sheep.* Victoria and Albert Museum (loaned from the Royal Collection), London.

LEONARDO DA VINCI, *Drawings.* A larger number of Leonardo's drawings survives than of any other great Italian artist of the 15th century. Their subject range is extraordinary and indicative of Leonardo's phenomenal curiosity and power of observation. His first dated drawing is 1473; most of the drawings shown can be dated between 1488 and 1519, the date of his death. The media include red chalk (he was probably the first to use this characteristic medium of the High Renaissance), black chalk, silver point on colored grounds and pen and ink. The two great collections of Leonardo's drawings are in the Royal Library, Windsor Castle, and the Ambrosiana Library, Milan. The following subjects are shown (unless otherwise indicated, the drawings are from the Royal Library, Windsor Castle): *Self-Portrait,* c. 1512, Royal Library, Turin; *Head of a Girl,* Royal Library, Turin; *Horse* (study for Sforza Monument) c. 1490; *Map of Diversion of the River Arno,* 1502; *Head of St. John; Calcula-*

tions, with sketch of a man; Mill wheel, Toothed wheel, Palace Tower, Domed Church, Stable, from Manuscript B, Institut de France, Paris; *Light Falling, Light Falling on Sphere,* from Manuscript A, Institut de France, Paris; *Profile of an Old Man, Waves, Whirlpool, Rocks, Storm Clouds, Trees, Acorns and Oak Leaves, Blackberries,* c. 1505-8, *Flowering Plant (Star of Bethlehem),* c. 1505-8, *Bird's Wing, Bird in Flight, Nude Man, rear view,* c. 1503-7, *Anatomical Drawings, Heart and Lungs,* c. 1510, *Baby in the Womb,* c. 1510-12, *Tongue, Old Men, Arm Ligaments, Deluge,* montage of details c. 1514.

6. Protest and Communication

The troubled world of the rise of Protestantism and the division of Christianity; of the invention of printing; of vicious religious wars and the humane spirits of Erasmus and Sir Thomas More; the art of Holbein and Dürer; the skepticism of Montaigne, and the heroic pessimism of Shakespeare.

"Whereas in talking about Italy one is concerned with the enlargement of man's spirit through the visual image, in the north one is chiefly concerned with the extension of his mind through the word. And this was made possible by the invention of printing. In the nineteenth century people used to think of the invention of printing as the lynchpin in the history of civilisation. Well, fifth century Greece and twelfth century Chartres and fifteenth century Florence got on very well without it—and who shall say that they were less civilised than we are. Still, on balance, I suppose that printing has done more good than harm."

During the greater part of the 15th and early 16th centuries, the arts in Northern Europe were strongly influenced by the Flemish masters. Foremost among these was Jan van Eyck (died 1441), whose *Giovanni Arnolfini and his Bride,* and *Ghent Altarpiece*—the greatest monument of Northern art of the period—Lord Clark has discussed in earlier programs. These masters, working in the newly developed oil medium, created a style of intense realism with an unmistakable Northern flavor. Their work, though carried on in a late Gothic atmosphere, represents a parallel to the revolutionary developments in music which were taking place at the same time and place, where a school of composers arose whose work dominated the field throughout Europe for a century.

The sculptures of the German master Tilman Riemenschneider (c. 1460-1531) show the transitional character of Northern art at this time. Still late medieval in feeling, and realized to the smallest detail in the manner of the Flemish, his work begins to show the influence of the Renaissance individualism. Yet it retains a curvilinear grace, and ornamental richness typical of the late Gothic.

One of the outstanding developments of this period in Northern Europe was, as Lord Clark says, the invention and use of printing. But along with this went a rich flowering of printmaking. Dürer, who appears importantly in this program, was following an already established tradition when he produced what have ever since been considered major works of art in a print medium. The printing press proliferated the work of many artists, both as individual works and as illustrations in books. Prints became increasingly influential on both painting and sculpture. Riemenschneider based several works of sculpture in large part on the delicate engravings of Martin Schongauer (c. 1430-91), who was himself a painter as well as a printmaker. Schongauer's style is also deeply influenced by that of the great Flemings, so his own influence, in turn, spread that of Flanders.

In later works, Riemenschneider reflects something of the style of Dürer, again through the medium of print. The development of printing and printmaking went hand in hand, and therefore had a profound effect on the course of the arts throughout the 15th century and long thereafter. John Singleton Copley (1738-1815), America's first great painter, for example, derived the poses, costumes and style of his early portraits from English prints after fashionable English portrait painters. During the 15th century the art of printing and of printmaking reached a state of such advanced development that there were virtually no changes in basic techniques until the 19th century.

With his emphasis on theory, as exemplified in his intense study of perspective, Dürer shows the influence of his trips to Italy, where he experienced the Renaissance in all its intensity at first hand. He was, then, the first of the Northern artists who can truly be said to belong to the Renaissance. He had an exact contemporary, however, about whom very little is known, who summed up the Late Gothic ideal in one of the most important, impressive, and moving works of art of its kind, the *Isenheim Altarpiece* (c. 1510-15, Unterlinden Museum, Colmar). The artist is Matthias Grünewald (c.

1470/80-1528). When closed the altar shows a *Crucifixion* so powerful as to be almost overwhelming. Entirely Northern in character and spirit, it has in its own way the high tragedy and heroism we associate with Michelangelo. Open, it shows dramatically contrasting idyllic scenes: on the left wing, the *Annunciation;* in the center, the *Nativity* with attendant musical angels; on the right wing a *Resurrection,* with Christ rising in glory from the tomb with an aura of gentle triumph to compensate for the painful expressiveness of the *Crucifixion.* Both Grünewald and Dürer died in the same year, the one bringing Gothic painting to a dramatic close, the other, the first of the new spirit and the new age.

Despite the horrors of the wars which troubled Europe during the 15th and 16th centuries, there were artists of great importance. Perhaps the most outstanding of these is the Netherlander, Pieter Bruegel the Elder (1530/35-69). Like so many, he visited Italy, but seems to have been more interested in the Alps than in anything else, because he returned with a sketchbook full of drawings which are among the finest Alpine views in art. His large canvasses depicting the Four Seasons are masterpieces of spacious landscape painting. *Winter: The Return of the Hunters* (Kunsthistorisches Museum, Vienna), is perhaps the most impressive of the series. But he also painted curious and moving symbolic pictures, like that illustrating the parable of *The Blind Leading the Blind,* in the National Museum at Naples, a pathetic commentary on human weakness and fallability.

The personal tastes of Francis I, the first Renaissance king of France and the last patron of Leonardo da Vinci, imported the ideals of the new movement into France during the 16th century. By this time, however, the phase known as Mannerism had begun in Italy, so it was largely a Mannerist style, transitional to the Baroque of the 17th century, that became the court style of France. It appears in the stucco-decorated galleries of the royal château at Fontainebleau, carried out by the Italian Francesco Primaticcio (1404-70), with other Italian assistants, and also in the paintings of the period. In the courtyard of the Louvre Palace in Paris, however, Pierre Lescot (c. 1515-78) realized a pure Renaissance facade based on the style of Bramante. In the Tomb (1563-70) of Henry II and wife, Catherine de' Medici, Germain Pilon (c. 1535-90), the most distinguished French sculptor of the period, achieved a synthesis of Mannerist and Renaissance qualities to produce an original work, in marble and bronze, of both grace and power, which looks forward to later French achievements in the following century. Like Lescot's facade, Pilon's sculptures strike a note of classicism which was to be the predominant quality of official French art during the next century and more.

As Lord Clark points out, England was a land apart during the disturbed and disturbing years of the ravaging of Europe by the Religious Wars. Yet England, too, had but only comparatively recently entered into a period of internal peace. Painting during the reign of Henry VIII was dominated by the German Hans Holbein (1497/8-1543), and other foreigners. Under Elizabeth came the English flowering of the Renaissance, but in literature rather than in the visual arts. It was a period of such intense richness that it included Edmund Spenser, Ben Jonson and Christopher Marlowe as well as many other poets and playwrights, who in a lesser period would have been considered of first rank. Its music also has great charm.

In Nicholas Hilliard (1547-1619) England produced a charming if minor painter, whose training as a goldsmith is reflected in the miniature scale and exquisite detail of his paintings. Queen Elizabeth herself preferred the flat, still largely medieval style of painting of an earlier period, so the Renaissance in visual arts and in architecture was not to reach England until the reign of the Stuart king Charles I.

Works of art as they appear in Program 6

TILMAN RIEMENSCHNEIDER, *Apostles*. c. 1500-06. Stone (a few examples in wood). Chapel of the fortress of Marienberg, Würzburg.

RAPHAEL, *Portrait of a Cardinal*. c. 1512. Panel, 31⅛x24″. Prado, Madrid.

ALBRECHT DÜRER, *Portrait of Oswolt Krell*. 1499. Panel, 19⅞ x 15⅝″. Alte Pinakothek, Munich.

QUENTIN MATSYS, *Portrait of Erasmus*. c. 1517. Panel transferred to canvas, 23¼x18⅛″. Galleria Nazionale, Rome.

PIETER BRUEGEL THE ELDER, *Peasant Dance*. c. 1567. Panel, 45x64½″. Kunsthistorisches Museum, Vienna.

ALBRECHT DÜRER, *King Plague (Crowned Death on a Thin Horse)*. 1505. Charcoal drawing. British Museum, London.

Magdalen College, Oxford University. Founded in 1458 by William of Waynflete, Bishop of Winchester, and built in 1475–1504. First Oxford college to admit commoners. Shown here: park, tower, courtyard.

HANS HOLBEIN, *Portrait of Erasmus.* 1523. Paper on panel, 14¼ x 11⅞". Kunstmuseum, Basel.

HANS HOLBEIN, *Portrait of Erasmus.* 1523. Panel, 16½x12½". Louvre, Paris.

HANS HOLBEIN, *Portrait of Erasmus.* c. 1523. Panel, 30x22". Collection Earl of Radnor, Longford Castle, Salisbury.

HANS HOLBEIN, *Portrait of Erasmus.* 1530. Panel, diameter 4¾". Öffentliche Kunstmuseum, Basel.

HANS HOLBEIN, *Self-Portrait.* 1542-43. Chalk drawing. Uffizi, Florence.

HANS HOLBEIN, *Portrait of Sir Thomas More.* 1527. Panel, 29¼ x 23¼". Frick Collection, New York.

Titlepage of *Utopia,* by Thomas More. First published (Latin) 1516.

HANS HOLBEIN, *Family of Sir Thomas More.* Pen drawing, 15¼x 20⅛". Kunstmuseum, Basel.

HANS HOLBEIN, *Portrait of Cecily Heron.* c. 1528. Chalk drawing. Windsor Castle. Third and youngest daughter of Sir Thomas More, b. 1507.

HANS HOLBEIN, *Portrait of Anne Cresacre.* c. 1528. Chalk drawing. Windsor Castle. Daughter of Edward Cresacre, b. 1512, married John More, only son of Sir Thomas More, 1529.

HANS HOLBEIN, *Portrait of Archbishop Warham.* c. 1528. Chalk drawing. Windsor Castle.

HANS HOLBEIN, *Portrait of Cardinal Fisher, Bishop of Rochester.* c. 1528. Chalk drawing. Windsor Castle. Chancellor of Cambridge University and Bishop of Rochester.

Plantin Press, Antwerp (now Plantin-Moretus Museum). Founded by Christophe Plantin (1514-89), who became a leading European printer by 1550. Plantin's books have admirable typography and accuracy.

Bible, printed by Johann Gutenberg. 1456. The first printed Bible; illuminations added by hand.

ALBRECHT DÜRER, *Portrait of Erasmus Writing.* 1526. Engraving.

HANS HOLBEIN, Marginal illustrations in Holbein's own copy of Erasmus's *Praise of Folly.* 1515. Pen drawings. Kunstsammlung, Basel. Shown here: Erasmus writing; Asses at divine service.

ALBRECHT DÜRER, *Self-Portrait*. 1498, Panel, 20½x16⅛″ Prado, Madrid.

ALBRECHT DÜRER, *Self-Portrait*. 1500. Panel, 27x19 3/5″. Alte Pinakothek, Munich.

ALBRECHT DÜRER, *Bathing Woman*. 1496. Pen drawing. Kunsthalle, Bremen.

ALBRECHT DÜRER, *Rhinoceros*. 1515. Pen drawing. British Museum, London.

ALBRECHT DÜRER, *Boats in Antwerp Harbor*. 1520. Pen drawing. Albertina, Vienna.

ALBRECHT DÜRER, *Walrus*. 1521. Pen and water color. British Museum, London.

ALBRECHT DÜRER, *Hare*. 1502. Pen and water color. Albertina, Vienna.

ALBRECHT DÜRER, *The Great Piece of Turf*. 1503. Watercolor. Albertina, Vienna.

ALBRECHT DÜRER, *Melencolia I*. 1514. Engraving.

ALBRECHT DÜRER, *Life of the Virgin*. 1501-4. Series of twenty woodcuts. Shown here: *Birth of the Virgin, Annunciation, Birth of Christ, Flight into Egypt* and *Sojourn of the Holy Family in Egypt*.

ALBRECHT DÜRER, *St. Jerome in His Cell*. 1514. Engraving.

ALBRECHT DÜRER, *Knight, Death and Devil*. 1513. Engraving.

ALBRECHT DÜRER, *Portrait of Erasmus*. 1521. Chalk drawing (unfinished). Louvre, Paris.

Ely Cathedral, England. Gothic. One of the largest cathedrals in England, built on the site of an abbey destroyed in 870. The architecture is of various Gothic styles. Shown here: the Lady Chapel, where heads of all but one of the 100 statues were knocked off during the Reformation.

LUCAS CRANACH, *Martin Luther with Monk's Tonsure*. 1520. Woodcut.

LUCAS CRANACH, *Martin Luther with Hat*. c. 1521. Engraving.

LUCAS CRANACH, *Martin Luther; Luther's Wife*. c. 1525. Panel, diameter of each, 4½″. Staatliche Museum, Weimar.

LUCAS CRANACH, *Martin Luther as Junker George*. c. 1521. Panel, 20¼x13¼″. Schlossmuseum, Weimar.

LUCAS CRANACH, *Martin Luther*. 1525. Panel, diameter 3¾″. Kunstmuseum, Basel.

LUCAS CRANACH, *Portrait of Luther's Father*. c. 1527. Tempera on paper, 7¾x7½″. Albertina, Vienna.

MARTIN LUTHER (translator), Title page of *Das Allte Testament* (Old

Testament), published 1522 in Wittenberg.

COVERDALE's Bible (in English), Title page, published 1535 in Cologne.

URS GRAF, *Soldier with Lance.* 1514. Pen drawing. Kunstmuseum, Basel.

NIKLAUS MANUEL DEUTSCH, *Martyrdom of the Ten Thousand.* 1517. Panel, 83½x57½". Gottfried Keller Stiftung, Berne.

ALBRECHT DÜRER, *The Apocalypse.* 1497-98. Series of 16 woodcuts. Shown here: *Four Horsemen of the Apocalypse; Opening of the Fifth and Sixth Seals.*

FRANÇOIS DUBOIS, *Massacre of St. Bartholomew's Day.* Panel, 16th century. Musée Cantonal des Beaux-Arts, Lausanne.

Montaigne's Tower, in Montaigne (near Bordeaux). The château where Montaigne was born, which had been the family seat for three generations. In the tower is Montaigne's book-lined study; the ceiling beams are inscribed with Greek and Latin quotations stressing man's frailty and ignorance, but including Terence's statement, "I am a man, and think that nothing human is foreign to me."

THOMAS DE LEU, *Portrait of Montaigne.* Third quarter of 16th century. Panel. Musée Condé, Chantilly.

Page from Montaigne's *Essais (Essays),* published 1588, containing diary additions in his own hand. Bibliothéque Municipale, Bordeau.

MASTER OF ST. SEBASTIAN, *St. Michael Defeating the Dragon.* c. 1500. Panel, 31x21¾". Musée Calvet, Avignon.

Little Moreton Hall, Cheshire. 1559-89. A moated house in the Elizabethan style. One of the best examples of half-timbered architecture.

Kirby Hall, Northamptonshire. 1570-75. Once the seat of the Earls of Winchilsea, built probably by Thomas Thorpe for Sir Humphrey Stafford. It was altered by Inigo Jones in 1638-40. Abandoned in 1823, the gardens have been restored.

7. Grandeur and Obedience

The splendors of Rome in the 17th century, the center of the Counter Reformation and the drama of the Baroque style, which, through the genius of Bernini and Borromini, and the pride and ambition of the papacy, re-established their city as the world's capital, and a Baroque masterpiece.

"Papal Rome—the Rome of Sixtus V—is the most grandiose piece of town planning ever attempted, and it anticipates by fifty years the great town plans of France and Germany. The amazing thing is that it was

done only a generation after Rome had been, as it seemed, completely humiliated—almost wiped off the map. The city had been sacked and burnt, the people of northern Europe were heretics, the Turks were threatening Vienna. It could have seemed to a far-sighted intellectual that the papacy's only course was to face the facts, and accept its dependence on the gold of America, doled out through Spain. Well, as you can see, this didn't happen. Rome and the Church of Rome regained many of the territories it had lost and became once more a great spiritual force."

The center of the flowering of the Baroque style was seventeenth-century Rome. Yet its beginnings may be found earlier in Florence, in the work of the two greatest Florentine artists, Leonardo da Vinci and Michelangelo. In 1503 the government of Florence commissioned of Leonardo a fresco of an event famous in Florentine history for the Grand Council Chamber in the Palace of the Signoria. Leonardo chose *The Battle of Anghiari*. Though not very important historically, no one disputed the choice of subject of one of the greatest giants of the world of art. Leonardo had always been interested in motion, especially anatomical motion, and in the horse as an embodiment of force, so he chose to paint a cavalry engagement.

The fresco was never finished. He had trouble with the experimental medium he used. But the cartoon was fully realized and was literally worn out by generations of students. It is best known through a copy made by the great northern Baroque master, Rubens, and through the many sketches Leonardo made in preparation for it. The subject was a mass of struggling horsemen, swirling in a violent circular motion, the animals participating as fiercely as their desperately fighting riders. In its dynamic motion in depth, intense emotionalism, chiaroscuro (dramatic use of light and shade), momentary quality, and compositon based upon a curving, spiraling, linear structure, it embodies all the principles of Baroque design found in the architecture of Bernini, and, even more, of Borromini, and the theatrical chiaroscuro of Caravaggio.

Michelangelo's designs for the Piazza di Campidoglio in Rome and, more dramatically, for the Laurentian Library in Florence also lead directly into the Baroque. In the Campidoglio the buildings are at a dynamic angle to one another in an anti-Renaissance fashion which was dictated by the structures already there. Michelangelo took advantage of this deliberately to create a theatrical setting,

St. Peter's and the Piazza in the 17th century (Engraving by Lieven Cruyl, 1694).

centered on the equestrian statue of Marcus Aurelius, the only work of its kind preserved from classical times because the people of the Dark Ages thought it to be Constantine, the first Christian Emperor, instead of the pagan philosopher emperor. In the surrounding facades Michelangelo used for the first time classical elements in a new and dramatic way: tall pilasters extending upward through two stories support a vast cornice, while columns flank the voids between the pilasters in the first story, creating a curious tension of architectural elements used in a new and emotional, rather than logical way. With the whole design integrated by the unifying pattern of the pavement, the result is like a stage set.

In the vestibule of the Laurentian Library in Florence, next door to San Lorenzo, Michelangelo took even greater liberties with the traditional elements of Classical architecture. Pediments are broken, pilasters taper downward instead of upward, columns—supporting members—are recessed in walls, thus apparently denying their function and used in an entirely new way. There are brackets which support nothing, and the complex and subtly curving stair is rather a marvelous piece of abstract sculpture than a functional element. The whole design has become a personal expression of great power, denying precedent and history, and looking directly through Mannerism forward to the passionate theatricality of the Baroque of the 17th century.

The classical strain continued, however, in the work of one of the most influential and successful architects of the 16th century, Andrea Palladio (1518-80) of Vicenza. Working in the tradition of Alberti, his logical, beautifully proportioned designs have an inevitability about them which is the result of a consummate command of the vocabulary of classical architecture. Also, Palladio's purpose was entirely different from that of Michelangelo. He was no genius, but he was a very gifted architect whose influence spread not only to England, where the designs of the first English Renaissance architect, Inigo Jones (1576-1652), are based on his, but also to the New World where he influenced the leading American architects like Charles Bulfinch (1763-1844) and Thomas Jefferson (1743-1826).

Palladio built numerous palaces and other buildings in and about Vicenza, superb villas on the Brenta, where Venetian aristocrats escaped the heat of summer, and the Venetian church of San Giorgio Maggiore, so familiar to the visitor who looks out from the

Piazza of San Marco to see it on the island across the intervening stretch of water picturesquely dotted with gondolas.

The Villa Rotonda in Vicenza is perhaps Palladio's most famous design. Outwardly square in plan, with columned porticoes on all four sides, it contains a circular interior, and is crowned with a dome. Dating from 1550, it was copied in England by Lord Burlington as Chiswick House, near London, in 1725. There were many publications of Palladio's designs which not only spread his fame but also his influence. Both Bulfinch and Jefferson, for example, owned copies.

The same Classical spirit prevailed in a major aspect of Baroque painting. While Caravaggio was dramatizing his compositions with the violent contrasts of light and shade and Peter Paul Rubens (1577-1640) was carrying out his vast commissions with superb command and vigor, a French expatriate, Nicolas Poussin (1593-1665), living in Rome, was recreating an ideal Classical world. The courtly art of France, dedicated to the propagandizing of the divinely sanctioned absolutism of the French monarch as exemplified at Versailles, for example, was very much an official art. But there was another and far more interesting aspect of French art which could not flourish amid the formalities of court life. Combining qualities from Raphael, Titian and classical reliefs, Poussin painted scenes from mythology and ancient history, sometimes of violent action, as in the *Rape of the Sabine Women* (c. 1636/7, Metropolitan Museum, New York), and sometimes, far more successfully to modern eyes, as in his *Landscape with the Burial of Phocion* (1648, Louvre, Paris), one of the most satisfying and lyric ideal landscapes ever produced—ordered, pervaded with calm and a vague melancholy.

Claude Lorraine (1600-82) suggests by his name the part of France from which he came, the province of Lorraine in eastern France, whose capital is the handsome city of Nancy. Of far more limited range than Poussin, and lacking his intellectual power, he carried the idyllic aspect of ideal classical landscape to a poetic perfection. Also from Lorraine was the fascinatingly individualistic painter Georges de la Tour (1593-1652). Borrowing the dramatic lighting and impenetrable shadows of Caravaggio, he composed pictures of intense stillness and compelling power. A *Madonna and Child,* for example, can scarcely be differentiated from a family scene in a peasant household, except by the rapt stillness which pervades the canvas and adds a further dimension of meaning. Compared to such works as these, the official art of France—that of the court and its limited circle of the privileged—becomes a stage set for the pomp of royalty, grand but dated, and lacking the qualities of continuing life and meaning which characterize the works of Poussin and de la Tour.

Works of art as they appear in Program 7

Piazza with Colonnade before St. Peter's, Rome. Gianlorenzo Bernini. 1656-67.

Santa Maria Maggiore, Rome. Built by Sixtus III, Pope from 432-40. One of the largest basilican churches in Rome. The original Ionic columns are of Hymettian marble.

Mosaics on nave wall of Santa Maria Maggiore, Rome. c. 430. *The Parting of Abraham and Lot; Pharaoh's Daughter; Passage of Jordan; Abraham and Melchisedec; City of Jerusalem.*

St. John Lateran, Rome. Originally a fourth-century basilica, present facade was erected 1733-36 according to plans by Alessandro Galilei. The obelisk was brought to Rome from the ancient Egyptian temple of Ammon at Karnak (Thebes),

Santa Trinità dei Monti, Rome. Begun 1495. Baroque facade possibly by Giacomo della Porta.

GIANLORENZO BERNINI, designer of travertine figures on roof of Colonnade, St. Peter's, Rome. 1656-67.

MICHELANGELO, *Last Judgment.* 1536-41. Fresco covering entire wall behind altar. Sistine Chapel in Vatican, Rome.

MICHELANGELO, *Creation of Adam.* 1508-12. Detail from fresco on ceiling of Sistine Chapel in Vatican, Rome.

TITIAN, *Paul III and His Nephews* (Ottavio and Alessandro Farnese). 1546. Oil, 78½ x49". Museo di Capodimonte, Naples.

TITIAN, *Portrait of Paul III* with "camauro." c. 1546. Oil on canvas, 41¾ x33½". Museo di Capodimonte, Naples.

SEBASTIANO RICCI, *Paul III Thinks of Convoking the Council of Trent,* part of a cycle of paintings with the history of Pope Paul III, founder of the Farnese dynasty. 1687-88. Oil on canvas, 47½ x71". Palazzo Farnese, Piacenza.

MICHELANGELO, The Capitol, on the Capitoline Hill (Campidoglio), Rome. 1546. Michelangelo remodelled the piazza on symmetrical lines, designed the palace facades on the three sides and superintended the erection of the approach stairway. Center: Palazzo del Senatore; left: present Capitoline Museum; right: Palazzo dei Conservatori.

MICHELANGELO, Fortification drawings. Pen and ink with wash. Casa Buonarroti, Florence.

St. Peter's, Rome. The project of building a new cathedral was begun by Pope Julius II in 1505 (see Old St. Peter's). Bramante began with a Greek-cross plan in 1506-13. Michelangelo finished much of the exterior at back and sides. (1546-64). Giacomo della Porta executed the dome using Michelangelo's design (1585-90). Carlo Maderno lengthened the nave to form a Latin cross and constructed the facade (1606-12). Bernini erected the colonnade forming the great piazza (1655-67).

MARTIN VAN HEEMSBERCK, The Four Piers of new St. Peter's and the remains of the northern transept of the old basilica. c. 1533. Print Room, Berlin-Dahlem.

MICHELANGELO, Basilica of St. Peter's, longitudinal section, Vatican, Rome. 1546-64. Engraved by Etienne Duperac, 1569.

GUERCINO, *Self-Portrait.* c. 1625. Oil on canvas, 25x18″. Uffizi, Florence.

GIANLORENZO BERNINI, *Self-Portrait.*c.1630. Oil. Galeria Borghese, Rome.

PETER PAUL RUBENS, *Self-Portrait.* 1623-24. Oil on wood, 33¾ x 24¾″. Windsor Castle.

GUIDO RENI, *The Madonna and Child Appearing to St. Filippo Neri.* Oil. Chiesa Nuova, Rome.

St. John of the Cross, Flemish school. 16th century.

FRANCESCO ZURBARAN, *St. Ignatius Loyola.* c. 1640. Oil. 39½ x39″. Hampton Court Palace, England.

PETER PAUL RUBENS, *St. Theresa's Vision of the Dove.* 1614. Panel, 17½ x23½″. Privately owned, formerly in the Reformed Carmelites at Brussels. Predella under retable shows *St. Theresa Kneeling Before Christ.*

DANIELE CRESPI, *St. Charles Borromeo at Supper.* c. 1627/8. Oil on canvas. Santa Maria della Passione, Milan.

GIOVANNI BATTISTA CRESPI, *St. Carlo Receiving Jesuits.* 1603. Oil on canvas. Duomo, Milan.

Workshop of Andrea della Robbia, *Adoration of Magi.* 1490-1500. Polychrome terra-cotta altarpiece, 7′8″x5′7″. Victoria and Albert Museum, London.

GIOVANNI BELLINI, *Madonna of the Pear,* c. 1475. Panel, 32½ x25¾″.

Accademia Carrara di Belle Arti, Bergamo.

FEDERICO BAROCCI, *Madonna del Popolo.* 1579. Panel, 11'9⅜"x 8'3¼". Uffizi, Florence.

8. The Light of Experience

The arts of seventeenth-century Holland, of Rembrandt, Hals and Vermeer; the philosophy of Descartes, "I think, therefore I am;" Sir Isaac Newton and his mathematical exposition of the laws which govern the universe; Sir Christopher Wren, scientist and architect; scientific discoveries and their implications for the age to come.

"All the greatest exponents of civilisation, from Dante to Goethe, have been obsessed by light—perhaps one could take it as the supreme symbol of civilisation. But in the seventeenth century light passed through a crucial stage. The invention of the lens was giving it a new range and power. Vermeer used the utmost ingenuity to make us feel the movement of light. He loved to show it passing over a white wall, and then, as if to make its progress more comprehensible, passing over a slightly crinkled map. And yet the scientific approach to experience ends in poetry and I suppose that this is due to an almost mystical rapture in the perception of light."

Seventeenth-century Rome remained the center of Baroque art, despite the fact that, except for Caravaggio, the three greatest Baroque painters—Rembrandt, Rubens and Velasquez—were not Italians and did not work there. The Baroque style generally prevailed throughout Europe from about 1600 to 1750, when it merged into the Rococo. From Rome emanated both the more classical architectural style of Bernini and the dramatic, almost eccentric style of his only rival, Borromini. In the north, the classical strain became the official style of France, producing the great royal château of Versailles, the Louvre and innumerable other examples.

The more romantic strain of Borromini better suited the German and Central European temperament, however, and resulted in such dramatic works as Johann Fischer von Erlach's (1656-1723) St. Charles Borromeus in Vienna, with its animated facade flanked by sculptured columns reminiscent of the Column of Trajan in Rome. The Kaisersaal in the Palace at Würzburg, mentioned by Lord Clark, is a climax of this aspect of the Baroque in the north. Balthasar Neumann (1687-1753) was a worthy successor to Fischer von Erlach. His fanciful, brilliant architectural design is carried into the ceiling painted by Giovanni Battista Tiepolo (1696-1770), last of the great Venetians, who continued the Baroque tradition, started in Rome, of painting the ceiling away with a vision of clouds, sky and assorted angels and deities. So complete is the illusion that the eye cannot discern where architecture ends and painting begins.

The greatest of the Roman Baroque painters was the tragic and disturbed genius, Caravaggio (1573-1610). During a short life constantly involved with violence, he somehow managed to produce a number of revolutionary works using chiaroscuro—the extreme contrast of light and shade—to produce dramatic effects. He used as models his neighbors in the questionable part of Rome in which he lived. But through the magic of light, he transformed his subjects into participants in religious events. So unorthodox was his approach that official judgment usually condemned his work. Yet that very unorthodoxy in the treatment of religious themes and the picaresque quality he gave to subjects of everyday life appealed to Protestant taste, especially in the Netherlands where through a group of his followers his influence was transmitted to Rembrandt. Indeed, there was scarcely an artist of the period anywhere who did not undergo some influence of the Caravaggesque, so pervasive was his style. During his short, desperate life he changed the course of Western painting.

Of the three greatest masters of Baroque painting outside Italy, two were northerners, both from the Low Countries, Rembrandt van Rijn (1606-69) from Protestant Holland, and Peter Paul Rubens (1577-1640) from Catholic Flanders. The third was Diego Velasquez (1599-1660) from Spain. Rembrandt was the son of a miller, while Rubens was an aristocrat, and Velasquez came from a solid family background and won honors, as did Rubens, as a successful court painter. By contrast, Rembrandt lived close to the Jewish quarter in Amsterdam, and, though he received many commissions, some from as far away as Sicily, painted mainly the subjects which he himself preferred, themes from the Bible, mostly from the Old Testament. He found among his Jewish neighbors those characterful examples of humanity which he rendered timeless through his revelation of inner spirit. Like Rubens, he was influenced by the almost all-prevailing dramatic contrast of light and dark of Caravaggio, as in his famous *Night Watch* (1642, Rijksmuseum, Amsterdam). But he increasingly used this contrast to add emotional depth to his interpretations. The tragedies of his own life—the loss of his young wife Saskia, the death of all their children save one in infancy and his bankruptcy—were translated in his art into a deeper sympathy and understanding of humanity. His self-portraits, such as that in the National Gallery, Washington, painted when he was fifty-three, show the evidence of these experiences. *The Return of the Prodigal Son,* both the print and the painting in Leningrad, show how he turned that experience into an expression which transcends his own period and rises above sectarian considerations to become universal in significance.

Rembrandt did not travel beyond Holland, but Rubens travelled a great deal during his long and full life. An early trip to Italy was decisive in developing his style; he absorbed the Italian tradition but made it entirely his own. He was early appointed court painter to the Spanish regent at Antwerp where he built a palatial house, set in spacious gardens, all according to his own design. There he painted indefatigably, surrounded by skilful pupils and assistants, and by the collection of art and antiquities which he prized. Vigorous, handsome and outgoing, he accomplished an unbelievable amount of work during his career, served as special ambassador on several occasions, visited the court of Charles I of England where he introduced the mature Baroque style, was knighted, and left his pupil, Anthony van Dyck (1599-1641) as court painter. He was undaunted by huge commissions, such as the series of very large paintings in the Luxembourg Palace in Paris, dating from the 1620's, celebrating the life of Marie de' Medici, Queen of Henry IV and mother of Louis XIII. Today we value more highly the sketches which he made entirely with his own hand as preliminary studies for such large commissions, and also the landscapes which he painted in later life, among the first and finest naturalistic scenes in art.

Rubens's visit to Spain on a diplomatic mission in 1628-29 was of profound influence on the development of Velasquez's art, because it led to his first trip to Italy, a major factor in the maturing of his style. Like Rubens, he studied the works of Titian, Caravaggio, and other Italians, but his own cool, reserved nature expressed itself in a style which reflects little evidence of such study. As court painter to Philip IV, he was consistently honored. He painted many superb portraits, but among his greatest works are *The Surrender of Breda,* painted at thirty-six in 1656, and *Las Meniñas* (*The Maids of Honor;* Prado, Madrid). The latter shows the artist at work in his studio, visited by the royal princess with attendants, while painting the king and queen, who are reflected in the mirror on the far wall in the background. It is an amazing painting, unified by light, and, though apparently completely informal in composition, actually most subtly constructed. The red cross of the order of Santiago on the artist's tunic is said to have been touched in by the king himself in honor of his bestowal of knighthood on the artist. Hung in a separate room in the Prado Museum in Madrid, the painting has a magical capacity to draw the observer into it unmatched by any other work of art.

It was Inigo Jones (1576-1652) who brought Renaissance architecture to England. Two visits to Italy made him a thorough Palladian. The results may be seen in his designs for the Banqueting Hall at Whitehall in London (1619-22), part of the scheme for a large Renaissance palace never further carried out, and the Queen's House at Greenwich (1616-35), an almost prismatic example of Palladian proportion and reserve. Jones also designed costumes and scenery for court masques, but, more importantly, prepared the way for Sir Christopher Wren (1632-1723), whose architectural career included the plan for the rebuilding of London after the great fire of 1666, and the many churches he designed to replace those burnt, each an extraordinary exercise in architectural ingenuity. His masterpiece is St. Paul's cathedral (1668-1711), recently cleaned of its years of grime and soot to emerge as a magnificently realized architectural concept.

Wren had a number of gifted assistants to carry out the demanding task of rebuilding burnt-out London. Outstanding among these was the playwright, Sir John Vanbrugh, whose weighty masterpiece is Blenheim Palace in Oxfordshire (begun 1705), the gift to the Duke of Marlborough, victor in the War of the Spanish Succession, an anticipation of the Romantic period in its dramatic silhouette and massing, its immense scale and theatrical effect to which all practicality was sacrificed.

Works of art as they appear in Program 8

JACOB VAN RUISDAEL, *View of Haarlem*. 1670. Canvas, 17x15". Rijksmuseum, Amsterdam.

GERRIT BERCKHEYDE, *The Groote Kerke (Great Church) at Haarlem*. 1696. Canvas, 27½x35½". Private Collection.

Frans Hals Museum, Haarlem.

FRANS HALS, *Assembly of Officers and Subalterns of Civil Guard of St. Adrian at Haarlem*. 1633. Canvas, 6'9"x11'. Frans Hals Museum, Haarlem.

FRANS HALS, *Banquet of Officers of the Civic Guard of St. Adrian at Haarlem*. 1627. Canvas, 72x105". Frans Hals Museum, Haarlem.

JAN DE BRAY, *Governors of the Children's Charity Home at Haarlem*. 1663. Canvas, 6'x8'1". Frans Hals Museum, Haarlem.

FRANS HALS, *Governors of the Old Men's Home*. 1664. Canvas, 5'8"x 8'5". Frans Hals Museum, Haarlem.

H. BALLONGIER, *Tulips*. 1639.   Colored engravings of tulips from E. van Sweertin's bulb catalogue and *Florilegum of Count John of Nassau*.

H. BOLLONGIER, *Tulips*. 1639. Oil, 26¾x21½". Rijksmuseum, Amsterdam.

PIETER DE HOOCH, *Interior with a Woman Drinking with Two Men and a Maidservant*. c. 1660. Panel, 29x25½". National Gallery, London.

PIETER DE HOOCH, *The Card Players*. c. 1670. Canvas, 26⅜x30¼". Louvre, Paris.

GABRIEL METZU, *A Visit to the Nursery*. 1661. Canvas, 30½x32". Metropolitan Museum of Art, New York.

PAULUS POTTER, *The Young Bull*. 1647. Canvas, 7'9½"x11'1½". Mauritshuis, The Hague.

REMBRANDT, *Self-Portrait*. c. 1661. Canvas, 36x30¼". Rijksmuseum, Amsterdam.

REMBRANDT, *Self-Portrait*. c. 1629. Panel, 14⅜"x11⅝". Mauritshuis, The Hague.

REMBRANDT, *Anatomy Lesson of Dr. Tulp*. 1632. Canvas, 66¾x 85¼". Mauritshuis, The Hague.

REMBRANDT, *Bathsheba*. 1654. Canvas, 56x56". Louvre, Paris.

REMBRANDT, *The Jewish Bride*. c. 1660. Canvas, 47x65½". Rijksmuseum, Amsterdam.

REMBRANDT, *Christ Healing the Sick*. 1649. Etching.

REMBRANDT, *The Prodigal Son*. 1636. Etching.

REMBRANDT, *Jews in a Synagogue*. 1648. Etching.

REMBRANDT, *The Money Lender (Beggars Receiving Alms at a Door)*. 1648. Etching.

REMBRANDT, *St. Peter's Prayer before the Raising of Tabitha*. 1654-55. Pen drawing and wash. Musée Bonnat, Bayonne.

REMBRANDT, *Christ Preaching the Forgiveness of Sins*. c. 1652. Etching.

FRANS HALS, *Portrait of René Descartes*. c. 1649. Canvas, 30x26¾".
Louvre, Paris.

Illustrations from René Descartes, *Principles of Philosophy*. Published
1644. Refraction of light, vortices, whirlpool.

LEONARDO DA VINCI, Whirlpool, detail of *Plan of an Embankment for
Diverting the Arno*. c. 1502. Pen drawing. Royal Library, Windsor
Castle.

JAN VERMEER, *View of Delft*. c. 1658. Canvas, 38¾x46". Mauritshuis,
The Hague.

JAN VERMEER, *Little Street in Delft*. c. 1658. Canvas, 21'¼x17¼".
Rijksmuseum, Amsterdam.

JAN VERMEER, *The Music Lesson*. c. 1656. Canvas, 29½x24⅝".
Buckingham Palace, London.

JAN VERMEER, *The Lace Maker*. c. 1664. Canvas, 9½x8¼". Louvre,
Paris.

JAN VERMEER, *Woman in Blue Reading a Letter*. After 1660. Canvas,
18¼x15½". Rijksmuseum, Amsterdam.

JAN VERMEER, *Woman Weighing Pearls*. c. 1665. Canvas, 16¾x15".
National Gallery of Art, Washington, D.C.

PIETER SAENREDAM, *Interior of Church of St. Cunera, Rhenen*. 1665.
Panel, 19¾x27". Mauritshuis, The Hague.

PIETER SAENREDAM, *Interior of the Groote Kerke, Haarlem*. Panel,
22½x31½". National Gallery, London.

PIETER SAENREDAM, *Interior of the Church of St. Odulphus, Assen-
delft*. Mid-17th century. Canvas, 19¾x30". Rijksmuseum, Amsterdam.

JAN VERMEER, *The Geographer*. c. 1668. Canvas, 21x18¼". Städelsches Kunstinstitut, Frankfurt.

JAN VERMEER, *The Artist's Studio*. c. 1665. Canvas, 47¼x39⅝".
Kunsthistorisches Museum, Vienna.

JAN VERMEER, *Soldier and Laughing Girl*. c. 1660. Canvas, 19⅞x
18⅛". Frick Collection, New York.

JAN VERMEER, *Girl Pouring Milk*. c. 1660. Canvas, 18x16¼". Rijksmuseum, Amsterdam.

JACOB VAN CAMPEN AND PIETER POST, Mauritshuis (house of John
Maurits of Nassau, Governor of Brazil), The Hague. 1633. Interior
rebuilt 1718, after fire. In 1820, became Royal Picture Gallery and
Museum.

JACOB VAN RUISDAEL, *Charles II Embarking at Scheveningen (A
Beach)*. After 1660. Canvas, 21x25½". Mauritshuis, The Hague.

JAN VAN DEN CAPPELLE, *Dutch Yacht with Barge Pulling Away*.

c. 1660-70. Panel, 33⅝ x45". National Gallery, London.

WILLEM VAN DE VELDE, *Dutch Yacht Surrounded by Smaller Vessels.* Second half of 17th century. Canvas, 35½ x49". National Gallery, London.

WILLEM VAN DE VELDE, *Small Dutch Vessel Close-Handed; A Gale.* Second half of 17th century. Canvas, 12½ x15½". National Gallery, London.

CHARLES BROOKING, *Shipping Becalmed in the Solent.* Mid-18th century. National Maritime Museum, Greenwich.

EDWARD PIERCE, *Bust of Christopher Wren.* 1673. Marble, height 26". Ashmolean Museum, Oxford.

Frontispiece of Isaac Newton's *Principia (Philosophiae naturalis principia mathematica).* Published 1687; English translation 1729.

Octagon Room at Royal Observatory, Greenwich, England. Engraving.

CHRISTOPHER WREN, Royal Observatory, Greenwich, England. 1705. Shown: exterior, interior of Octagon Room.

John Flamsteed, Instruments for Astronomical and Nautical Observation. Shown: quadrant, telescope. Octagon Room, Flamsteed House, Greenwich Observatory, Greenwich.

Seventeenth-century scientific instruments: Italian telescope and Leeuwenhoek's microscope (copy) in Science Museum, South Kensington, London; astrolabe, armillary sphere, equinoctial dial and diptych dial in Octagon Room, Royal Observatory, Greenwich.

CHRISTOPHER WREN, Naval Hospital, now Royal Naval College; Royal Observatory; Queen's House (by Inigo Jones), now National Maritime Museum; Greenwich.

JAMES THORNHILL, *Apotheosis of William and Mary.* Ceiling of Painted Hall (formerly dining hall). Early 18th century. Naval Hospital, Greenwich.

WENZEL HOLLAR, *St. Paul's before the Great Fire of London.* 1666. Engraving.

CHRISTOPHER WREN, *Dome for Old St. Paul's.* 1665. Drawing. All Soul's College, Oxford.

Great Fire of London, 1666. Canvas. London Museum, London.

CHRISTOPHER WREN, The thirty "City" Churches, London. Shown: St. Mary-le-Bow, c. 1680; St. Andrew's, Holborn, 1684-90; St. Bride's, 1670-84.

CHRISTOPHER WREN. St. Paul's Cathedral. 1668-1711. London.

9. The Pursuit of Happiness

The age of the Rococo, an age of music, carefree life, and of great art; the music of Bach, Mozart and Handel; the painting of Fragonard and Watteau; the spectacular architecture of Balthasar Neumann and the brothers Zimmerman; a period of intimacy and of flirtation; a happy, fleeting moment between Baroque grandeur and the Age of Reason.

"This programme is primarily about music; and some of the qualities of eighteenth-century music—its melodious flow, its complex symmetry, its decorative invention—are reflected in its architecture; but not its deeper appeal to emotions. And yet the Rococo style has a place in civilisation. Serious-minded people may call it shallow and corrupt; well, the founders of the American constitution, who were far from frivolous, thought fit to mention the pursuit of happiness as a proper aim for mankind, and if ever this aim has been given visible form it is in Rococo architecture—the pursuit of happiness and the pursuit of love."

Throughout the period of the Baroque there ran the two strains of the more classical, represented by the architecture of Gianlorenzo Bernini (1598-1680)—as, for example, in the colonnaded piazza in front of St. Peter's in Rome—and the more fanciful, often anti-classical style of Francesco Borromini (1599-1667), whose Roman churches of Sant' Agnese (begun 1653), with its undulating facade, and Sant' Ivo (begun 1642), with its curious spiral tower, Lord Clark illustrates. This duality was paralleled in painting by the dispute between what the French called the Rubenists and the Poussinists, those who emphasized color and those who emphasized form. The Rococo style, which intermingles with the late Baroque, represents a victory for the more fanciful and colorful. It also emphasized intimacy of scale with far less of the parade of the Baroque except in court circles. Sentiment took precedence over reason. There were elements of the erotic and the melancholy inherent in it, as Lord Clark brings out in characterizing Watteau as *the* Rococo painter. Venus and Pan and the classical deities reappeared in design. The small scale, exquisitely modeled sculptures of the French artist, Claude Michel Clodion (1738-1814), like his *Satyr and Bacchante* (c. 1775, Metropolitan Museum, New York), and the canvases of Jean Honoré Fragonard (1732-1806) whose light color scheme was perfect for the nude bathing girls and amorous couples and garden parties he painted so deliciously. The delicacy of the medium of porcelain lent itself aptly to the expression of the Rococo spirit with charming figurines of Harlequins and shepherdesses, and characters from the Italian comedy then so popular.

After the death of Louis XIV in 1714, the court was no longer centered at Versailles. The nobility built town houses in Paris which reflected the new taste and spirit in greater simplicity of design and greater delicacy in decoration, with the emphasis on simplicity over formality. It was this new pattern of life, of intimate parties, of houses with a new sense of privacy, that so impressed such visiting Americans to Paris as Thomas Jefferson, and influenced the changes he made in his own house, Monticello, then in process of construction in Virginia.

Because of its qualities of color and also its necessarily smaller scale, pastel became a favorite Rococo medium. It was widely used, especially for portraiture, where the works of Quentin de Latour (1704-88) and of Jean Baptiste Perronneau (1715?-83), examples of which appear in the next program, are outstanding and full of vivid characterization. Their frequently sketchlike quality is shared by the painting of the Venetian, Francesco Guardi (1712-93), whose decorative fantasies were as popular as the supremely accurate city scenes of his contemporaries Antonio Canaletto (1697-1768) and the latter's nephew and pupil, Bernardo Bellotto (1720-80), through whose paintings of various European cities, including London, which Canaletto visited in the 1740's and 50's, we have wonderfully accurate representations of major European cities during the Rococo period. Bellotto's views of Warsaw are so detailed that they were used in the recent reconstruction of the Old City after the last war.

Perhaps because Late Gothic tendencies lingered longer there, the German-speaking countries, especially to the South, excelled in the fanciful Rococo style which, in elaboration of detail, resembles late German Gothic. The French origins of the style are clear in the work of François de Cuvilliés (1698-1767) whom Lord Clark mentions as both court dwarf and court architect to the Elector Max Emmanuel of Bavaria. Cuvilliés, born in Hennegau, Belgium, studied in Paris, and in the small royal hunting lodge, the Amalienburg, built for the electress on the grounds of the Palace of Nymphenburg in 1724, created one of the purest examples of the Rococo style.

The Emperor Frederick the Great, inspired by his admiration for all things French, introduced the Rococo in Prussia, the outstanding examples being the interiors he is said to have designed himself for the royal palace of Sans Souci at Potsdam in 1744-47. The Zwinger Palace in Dresden, the result of the collaboration (1711-22) of the architect Matthaus Pöppelmann (1662-1736) and the sculptor Balthasar Permoser (1651-1732), looks like a fantastic setting for an operatic ball, and is the essence of the Rococo spirit. The interior of the Bavarian pilgrimage church of the Wies (1745-54) designed by Dominikus Zimmermann (1685-1766), with stucco work and frescoes by his elder brother, Johann Baptist (1680-1758), is surpassed only by Balthasar Neumann (1687-1753) in his incomparable church of the Fourteen Saints, Vierzehnheiligen, with its flowing sense of space and upward movement. It is such works as these which form the counterpart to the musical achievements which Lord Clark discusses so eloquently in this program.

Works of art as they appear in Program 9

Schloss Nymphenburg, west of Munich. Extensive group of buildings erected 1663-1728. Great Hall decorated by J. B. Zimmermann (1756). In the large park beyond the Schloss are elaborate gardens and buildings, including the Amalienburg (see below).

The Louvre, Paris. French palace (now museum) built from 16th to 19th centuries. Shown here: East facade by CLAUDE PERRAULT (1670); west facade partly by PIERRE LESCOT (c. 1550).

FRANCESCO BORROMINI, Sant'Ivo della Sapienza, Rome. 1642-50.

FRANCESCO BORROMINI and CARLO RAINOLDI. Sant'Agnese in Piazza Navona. Begun 1652. Rome.

JOHANN MICHAEL FISCHER, Benedictine Abbey Church, Ottobeuren (Bavaria). 1736-66. Nave with baptismal font, illusionistic wall paintings, pulpit, gold decorations, stucco figures, frescoes.

Organ built by CHRISTIAN MULDER, 1735-38, in Groote Kerke, Haarlem. Great example of Baroque organ building, with so-called bass towers (groups of long bass organ pipes rising from levels of different heights).

E.G. HAUSMANN, *Portrait of Johann Sebastian Bach.* c. 1740. Canvas. Private Collection.

BALTHASAR NEUMANN, Church of the Vierzehnheiligen (Fourteen Saints), Abbey of Langheim, Germany. 1743-72. One of the best illustrations of the transition from Baroque to Rococo. Shown here: sculptures of cherubs, St. Erasmus, St. Eustachius, St. Christopher;

pulpit, high altar.

LOUIS FRANÇOIS ROUBILIAC, *The Vauxhall Handel.* 1738. Marble, slightly under lifesize. Victoria and Albert Museum, London.

BALTHASAR NEUMANN, Bishop's Palace (Residenz), Würzburg, 1720-44. Large palace and gardens; outstanding is the huge staircase, with ceiling by Tiepolo; White Room with elaborate stucco ornament and chandelier.

GIOVANNI BATTISTA TIEPOLO, *Olympus and the Four Continents,* ceiling fresco of staircase, Bishop's Palace, Würzburg. 1751-53. Seen here: self-portrait; portrait of his son Giovanni Domenico; portrait of Balthasar Neumann and associates; personifications of America, Africa, Asia.

GIOVANNI BATTISTA TIEPOLO, *Christ Carrying the Cross.* 1749. Canvas. Sant'Alvise, Venice.

ANTOINE WATTEAU, *Champs Elysées (Elysian Fields).* 1717-21. Panel, 12½ x 76⅜". Wallace Collection, London.

ANTOINE WATTEAU, *Women's Heads.* Chalk drawing. British Museum, London.

ANTOINE WATTEAU, *Heads.* Chalk drawing. British Museum, London.

ANTOINE WATTEAU, *Fêtes Vénitiennes.* 1716-19. Canvas, 22x18". National Gallery of Scotland, Edinburgh.

ANTOINE WATTEAU. *Gilles.* 1716-20. Canvas, 6¾ x 4'11". Louvre, Paris.

ANTOINE WATTEAU. *Departure from the Island of Cythera.* 1717. Canvas, 4'3"x6'4½". Louvre, Paris.

ANTOINE WATTEAU, *Departure from the Island of Cythera.* 1717. 4'3"x6½'. Gemaldegalerie, Berlin-Dahlem.

ANTOINE WATTEAU, *Les Charmes de la Vie (The Music-Party).* c. 1719. Canvas, 25½ x 36¼". Wallace Collection, London.

ANTOINE WATTEAU, *The Music Lesson.* c. 1718. Panel, 7x9". Wallace Collection, London.

ANTOINE WATTEAU, *Gilles and His Family.* c. 1718. Panel, 10⅜ x 8". Wallace Collection, London.

Music Room from Norfolk House. 1756. Victoria and Albert Museum, London. Matthew Brettingham (1699-1769) was the architect of Norfolk House which was owned by the Dukes of Norfolk from 1725-1937. In 1737-41 it was lent to Frederick, Prince of Wales, and in a house behind the later mansion (built 1742-52, demolished 1938) George III was born in 1738.

DOMINIKUS ZIMMERMANN. Pilgrimage Church "Die Wies." 1745-54.

Bavaria, Germany. Shown here: exterior; interior with cherubs, organ, carved wood pews.

FRANÇOIS DE CUVILLIÉS, Amalienburg. 1734-39. In park of Schloss Nymphenburg, near Munich. It was built for the Electress Maria Amalia, wife of the Elector Karl Albrecht of Bavaria. The stucco is by J. B. Zimmermann and the carving by J. Dietrich. It contains the famed Hall of Mirrors, shown here, and the Yellow Room. The pavilion represents the culmination of Cuvilliés's art and is one of the earliest and most perfect examples of German Rococo.

JOSEPH LANGE, *Portrait of Wolfgang Amadeus Mozart.* c. 1782. Canvas (unfinished), 12½ x 11″. Mozarteum, Salzburg.

FRANÇOIS DE CUVILLIÉS, Residenz Theatre. 1751-53. Munich. Shown here: Rococo decoration of caryatids, satyrs, etc., on balcony and boxes.

10. The Smile of Reason

The Age of Reason, of Voltaire and his wit and passion for justice, of the creation of encyclopedias, of the salon with its brilliant conversation; an age in which the pursuit of reason led to revolution; an age of the accomplished sculpture of Houdon and the painting of Jacques Louis David; the era which saw the birth of the United States, whose foundation in the principles of the Age of Reason is reflected in the career, both political and architectural, of Thomas Jefferson.

"The smile of reason. . . . It seems to us shallow—we've got into deep water in the last fifty years. We feel that people ought to be more passionate, more convinced—or as the current jargon has it, more committed.

The smile of reason may seem to betray a certain incomprehension of the deeper human emotions; but it didn't preclude some strongly held beliefs—belief in natural law, belief in justice, in toleration, in humanitarianism. Not bad. The philosophers of the enlightenment pushed European civilisation some steps up the hill, and in theory, at any rate, this gain was consolidated throughout the nineteenth century."

This program deals with that aspect of the 18th century which has often been called the Age of Reason. The latter part of the same century also saw the birth of Romanticism, but this program treats the classical aspects of the period, even though Blenheim (1705-26), the vast country house which Sir John Vanbrugh (1664-1726) built for the Duke of Marlborough, has a theatrical quality which gives a foretaste of the Romantic movement.

About 1720, Lord Burlington (1694-1753), whose Chiswick House Lord Clark illustrates, introduced the Palladian tradition into England, which was not only to prove popular there throughout the greater part of the century, but was also to spread to the American colonies, where Thomas Jefferson's Monticello is an outstanding example. A Scot, Robert Adam, introduced a more classical element with his publication of drawings of the ruins of Diocletian's palace at Spalato. The discoveries of the remains of Herculaneum and Pompcii, and James Stuart and Nicholas Revett's magnificent volumes on *The Antiquities of Athens*, published in 1762, further fed the increasing stream of classicism. Robert Adam's own architecture, such as Kedleston Hall in Derbyshire or Osterley Park in Middlesex (illustrated in the 12th program), show his combination of uncluttered forms with smaller scale interior decoration derived from his archeological studies, and his superb qualities as both architect and decorator.

English painting was dominated at this time by Sir Joshua Reynolds (1723-92), first president of the Royal Academy, and the more gifted Thomas Gainsborough (1727-88), who, unlike Reynolds, did not confine himself primarily to portraiture, but also painted brilliant landscapes influenced by Rubens and the Dutch, but with an inimitable touch and technical mastery of paint the more pedestrian Reynolds could never match. The Americans, Benjamin West and John Singleton Copley, entered the London scene around mid-century, but their works belong rather to the beginnings of Romanticism, in which they were both pioneers, than with the classical tradition.

In France the Panthéon in Paris (1755-92), designed by Jacques Germain Soufflot (1713-81), remains an outstanding example of the classical approach. Its almost blank walls give it an austere substance and solidity, and lead up to a dome on a columnar drum, which, curiously, is derived from that by Wren for St. Paul's in London.

The leading French painter in this tradition is Jacques Louis David (1748-1825), whose hard-edge, sculpturesque paintings often suggest classical reliefs. His dominance of French painting during the period represented a definite victory for the Poussinists. His follower, Jean Auguste Dominique Ingres (1780-1867), a great draftsman, continued the classical tradition far into the ensuing

Romantic age. The outstanding French sculptor was Jean Antoine Houdon (1741-1828), whose famous *Voltaire* opens the program, and whose *Washington*, in Jefferson's Capitol at Richmond, is also illustrated.

David showed a marvelous capacity for rapid adjustment to the swiftly changing political tides of the century in France. A passionate partisan of the French Revolution, for which he can be considered almost the official painter, he unhesitatingly turned to the glorification of Napoleon as a successor of the emperors of old, and became as much the official painter of the Empire as he had been of the Revolution.

THOMAS JEFFERSON'S MONTICELLO

After the winning of American independence a predominantly Georgian style in architecture, with strong accents of Palladianism —as may be seen in Jefferson's Monticello, and also at Washington's Mount Vernon—was replaced by the Federal style, best exemplified by the works of Samuel McIntire (1757-1811) in Salem, Massachusetts, and those of the far more influential Charles Bulfinch (1763-1844) of Boston whose Boston State House and many houses on Beacon Hill in that city show the slenderer forms, influenced by

Robert Adam, which characterized the Federal style. Later Bulfinch turned to the greater simplicity and monumentality of form which appears in his mature designs, and which were broadcast throughout the country by the many builders' manuals published by his pupil and follower, Asher Benjamin. In the meantime, however, in basing his design for the Virginia state Capitol (completed 1789) uncompromisingly on the antique model of the temple called the Maison Carrée at Nîmes, Thomas Jefferson in 1798 formally introduced the style which was to prevail, not only in America, but in Europe as well—the Classic Revival. The Church of the Madeleine in Paris (1807) was to be the next important example of this international style.

In American painting, Copley's and then Gilbert Stuart's (1755-1828) practice dominated portraiture and maintained a very high level of quality. Stuart had had the benefit of study in London with his countryman, Benjamin West, Reynolds' successor as President of the Royal Academy. But Copley forged his own masterful style from his own determination and natural gifts. John Trumbull (1756-1843), recorded scenes from the major battles of the Revolutionary War in brilliant small canvasses, and, between the time that Copley left for London on the eve of the outbreak of war and the return from Europe of Stuart in 1793, the versatile Charles Willson Peale (1741-1827) ably filled the gap, and also established in Baltimore the first museum based on modern systematic principles.

It was an able practitioner of the classical style and a follower of Jefferson and Bulfinch, Robert Mills (1781-1855) who designed that gigantic obelisk, the Washington Monument, which appears toward the end of the program. Its construction, like that of the national Capitol, was interrupted by the Civil War. Charles Bulfinch completed the first version of the Capitol in Washington in 1830, unifying the work of four previous architects, and creating a whole of real distinction. In later enlargements, wings were extended at either end of the building by another accomplished classicist, Thomas U. Walters (1804-87), who designed its handsome cast-iron dome as well, the construction of which was also interrupted by the Civil War. It was Jefferson who was largely responsible for commissioning the French officer-engineer, Pierre Charles L'Enfant, to create the master plan for the new Federal city, a plan of classical flavor with a definite French accent.

VICTOR LOUIS, Théâtre Française. 1786-90. Home of the Comédie Française. The corridor is decorated with 18th- and 19th-century statues and busts of famous authors. Shown: *Bust of Marivaux.*

JEAN ANTOINE HOUDON, *Statue of Voltaire.* 1781. Marble, height 47". Théâtre Française, Paris.

NICOLAS DE LARGILLIERE, *Portrait of Fontenelle.* Early 18th century. Canvas. Museum of Chartres.

ALEXANDRE ROSLIN, *Portrait of Jean François Marmontel.* 1767. Canvas, 25½"x21". Louvre, Paris.

MAURICE QUENTIN DE LATOUR, *Self-Portrait.* 1751. Pastel, 25¼ x 21⅝". Museum of Picardy, Amiens.

MAURICE QUENTIN DE LATOUR, *Portrait of Marie Fel.* 1757. Pastel, 12½x9½". Musée Lecuyer, Saint-Quentin.

MAURICE QUENTIN DE LATOUR, *Self-Portrait.* Pastel, 22x17½". Louvre, Paris.

MAURICE QUENTIN DE LATOUR, *Portrait of Mlle. Dangeville.* Preparatory sketch, pastel, 12¼x9½". Musée Lecuyer, Saint-Quentin.

MAURICE QUENTIN DE LATOUR, *Portrait of Prosper Jolyot de Crevillon.* Preparatory sketch, pastel, 12¼x8½". Musée Lecuyer, Saint-Quentin.

MAURICE QUENTIN DE LATOUR, *Portrait of Jean le Rond d'Alembert.* 1753. Pastel, 21⅝x18". Louvre, Paris.

MAURICE QUENTIN DE LATOUR, *Portrait of Voltaire.* (copy; original painted 1736). Château de Ferney, France.

Voltaire in the Bastille, 18th century. Engraving. Bibliothèque Nationale, Paris.

SIR JOHN VANBRUGH, Blenheim Palace. 1705-20. The most monumental mansion in England, Baroque in style. Presented to the Duke of Marlborough after his victory at Blenheim, Bavaria, during the War of the Spanish Succession.

SIR GODFREY KNELLER, *Portrait of Sir John Vanbrugh.* c. 1715. Canvas, 36x27". National Portrait Gallery, London.

MICHAEL DAHL (attr. to), *Portrait of Lord Burlington.* c. 1725-30. Canvas. Private Collection.

LORD BURLINGTON and WILLIAM KENT. Chiswick House, Chiswick, near London. Begun 1725. Modeled after Italian villas by Palladio, chiefly the Villa Rotonda in Vicenza. Compact, simple and geometric in style. Marked the beginning of the Palladian revival in England.

WILLIAM HOGARTH, *The Orgy,* scene iii from *The Rake's Progress.* 1732-33. 24½x29½". Sir John Soane's Museum, London.

WILLIAM HOGARTH, *The Gaming House,* scene vi from *The Rake's Progress.* 1732-33. Canvas, 24½x29½". Sir John Soane's Museum, London.

WILLIAM HOGARTH, *The Polling,* scene iii from *The Election.* 1754. Canvas, 40x50". Sir John Soane's Museum, London.

WILLIAM HOGARTH, *Chairing the Member,* scene iv from *The Election.* 1754. Canvas, 40x50". Sir John Soane's Museum, London.

ARTHUR DEVIS, *The John Orde Family.* 1750-55. Canvas, 37x37⅛". Paul Mellon Collection, Upperville, Virginia.

THOMAS GAINSBOROUGH, *Mr. and Mrs. Robert Andrews.* c. 1748-50. Canvas, 27½x47". National Gallery, London.

WILLIAM HOGARTH, *A Midnight Modern Conversation.* 1734. Engraving. British Museum, London.

JEAN FRANÇOIS DE TROY, *A Reading from Molière.* c. 1730. Marquess and Marchioness of Cholmondeley, London.

Salon, in the Musée Carnavalet, Paris. 18th century.

MICHEL BARTHELEMY OLLIVIER, *Supper with the Prince de Conti in the Temple,* 1766. Versailles.

Portrait of Mme. du Deffand. 18th century. Pastel sketch. Spinal Museum.

HUBERT ROBERT, *Mme. Geoffrin Eating While Her Servant Reads to Her.* c. 1772. Canvas, 26x23". Louvre, Paris.

JEAN FRANÇOIS GILLE COLSON, *Portrait of Mme. Geoffrin.* 18th century. Canvas. Musée Carnavalet, Paris.

JEAN-BAPTISTE PERRONEAU, *Portrait of Mme. de Sorquainville.* 1749. Canvas. Louvre, Paris.

LOUIS MICHEL VANLOO, *A Cup of Chocolate.* 18th century. Canvas. Versailles.

Versailles. Palace of Versailles, eleven miles from Paris, begun in 1669 by Le Vau for Louis XIV. Constructed around an old hunting château (1624-26) built for Louis XIII. Later, Louis XIV employed Jules Hardouin Mansart to extend the palace, forming a building more than a quarter of a mile long. Other portions were added in 1756 for Louis XV. The interior apartments are sumptuously decorated; the most famous of these, the Hall of Mirrors, was decorated by Le Brun in 1680. The magnificent formal gardens were laid out by André Le Nôtre. The royal residence was typical of the Age of Louis XIV both in the magnitude of its layout and the enormous expenditure of money and labor involved.

CARTELLIER AND PETITOT, *Equestrian Statue of Louis XIV*. Courtyard of the Ministers, Versailles.

JEAN BAPTIST SIMEON CHARDIN, *The Morning Toilet*. c. 1740. Canvas, 19¼ x 15⅜". National Museum of Stockholm.

J. B. S. CHARDIN, *The Scullery Maid*. 1738. Canvas, 17¾ x 14¼". Hunterian Museum, University of Glasgow.

J. B. S. CHARDIN, *The Cellar Boy*. 1738. Canvas, 17⅜ x 13¾". Hunterian Museum, University of Glasgow.

J. B. S. CHARDIN, *The Kitchen Maid*. 1738. Canvas, 17⅜ x 13⅜". Kress Collection, National Gallery of Art, Washington, D.C.

J. B. S. CHARDIN, *The Governess*. 1739. Canvas. National Gallery, Ottawa.

MICHEL BARTHELEMY OLLIVIER, *Tea in the English Manner in the Salon of the Four Mirrors at the Temple with the Court of the Prince de Conti*. 1766. Player at the harpsichord is the young Mozart. Louvre, Paris.

Family Concert in a Salon. 18th century. Canvas. Private Collection. Paris.

JEAN-MICHEL MOREAU LE JEUNE, *Don't Be Afraid, Dear Friend*. c. 1780. Engraving from a series, *The Monument of Costume*, by Moreau le Jeune and other artists.

FRANÇOIS BOUCHER, *La Toilette*. 18th century. Canvas. Private Collection.

FRANÇOIS BOUCHER, *Le Déjeuner*. 1739. Canvas, 32¼ x 25⅝". Louvre, Paris.

FRANÇOIS BOUCHER, *Portrait of Mme. Boucher on a Sofa*. 1743. Canvas, 22½ x 26⅞". Frick Collection, New York.

ANICET LEMONNIER, *The Salon of Mme. Geoffrin*. 1814. Canvas. Musée des Beaux Arts, Rouen.

LOUIS MICHEL VANLOO, *Portrait of Diderot*. 1767. Canvas. 32x25½". Louvre, Paris.

Encyclopédie; ou Dictionnaire raisonné des sciences, des arts et des métiers. 1751-72. Twenty-eight volumes, of which 11 were devoted to plates illustrating the industrial arts, compiled by Diderot. Among the plates shown: polishing of wood, dyeing of wool for the Gobelin tapestries.

WRIGHT OF DERBY, *Experiment on a Bird in the Air Pump*. c. 1767-

68. Canvas, 72x96". Tate Gallery, London.

WRIGHT OF DERBY, *A Philosopher Giving a Lecture on the Orrery.* c. 1764-66. Canvas, 58x80". Derby Museum and Art Gallery.

JEAN MARC NATTIER, *Portrait of Joseph Bonnier de la Mosson.* 1745. Canvas, 54¼x41½". National Gallery of Art, Washington, D.C.

JACQUES LOUIS DAVID, *Portrait of Antoine Laurent Lavoisier.* 1788. Canvas, 100x76". Rockefeller University, New York.

JAMES TASSIE, *Profile Portrait Plaque of Adam Smith.* Medallion, plaster, 4x3". Scottish National Portrait Gallery, Edinburgh.

ALLAN RAMSAY, *Portrait of David Hume.* Private Collection, Edinburgh.

ALLAN RAMSAY, *Portrait of David Hume.* 1766. Canvas, 30x25". Scottish National Portrait Gallery, Edinburgh.

ROBERT AND JAMES ADAM, New Town of Edinburgh. Aerial view shown of circuses and closeup of Charlotte Square. Begun 1768.

GEORGE MEIKLE KEMP, Monument to Sir Walter Scott. 1840-44. Edinburgh.

Ravenshead Glassworks. 18th century. Canvas. Marshall Spink, Ltd.

WRIGHT OF DERBY, *Arkwright's Mill at Night.* c. 1782-83. Canvas, 34x45". Private Collection.

Château of Ferney. Home of Voltaire, 1758-78, on the French shore of Lake Geneva, about four miles from Geneva. Voltaire built the wings of the château and a chapel on the grounds at Ferney.

Full-length Portrait of Voltaire in Plumed Hat. 1772. Drawing. Château de Ferney.

JEAN HUBER, *Voltaire, in Cap, Wearing Blue Coat;* in background, view of Ferney. c. 1750-75. Drawing. Château de Ferney.

JEAN HUBER, *Voltaire Playing Checkers with Friends.* c. 1750-75. Wash drawing. British Museum, London.

Calas Family in Jail. Second half 18th century. Engraving.

JEAN HUBER. *Voltaire Having Coffee with a Lady.* Third quarter 18th century. Wash drawing. British Museum, London.

JEAN HUBER, *Portrait of Voltaire in Bonnet Hat.* Third quarter 18th century. British Museum, London.

Allegorical Engraving of Voltaire and Paris: Voltaire Being Crowned With a Laurel Wreath. c. 1778. Engraving by Dupin after drawing by Desrais.

Voltaire Being Crowned in a Box at the Théâtre Française. c. 1778. Print.

Voltaire's Bust being Crowned on the Stage of the Théâtre Française.

c. 1778. Engraving by C.-E. Gaucher, after drawing by Moreau le Jeune.

Apotheosis of Voltaire, July 11, 1791. c. 1791. Engraving by Berthault after drawing by Prieur.

Voltaire in Study with a Priest. Second half 18th century. Engraving by J. Lante, after drawing by Locatellus.

JACQUES LOUIS DAVID, *Self-Portrait.* Canvas, 32x25". 1794. Louvre, Paris.

JACQUES LOUIS DAVID, *The Oath of the Horatii.* 1784. Canvas, 10'10" x14'. Louvre, Paris.

JEAN-HONORE FRAGONARD, *The Swing.* Canvas, 31⅞x25⅝". Wallace Collection, London.

JACQUES LOUIS DAVID, *Brutus and His Dead Son.* 1787. Canvas, 10'8"x14". Louvre, Paris.

GEORGE CATLIN, Indian paintings, c. 1832. Smithsonian Institution, Washington, D.C. Shown are: *Portrait of Little Wolf; Portrait of Buffalo Back Fat, Chief of the Blackfeet; Buffalo Chase (I); Buffalo Chase (II); Artist and Guide Approaching Buffalo under Wolf Skins.*

THOMAS JEFFERSON, *Monticello.* Begun 1770, with additions throughout Jefferson's life. Designed entirely by Jefferson, it was his home for 56 years. Building materials prepared on the estate; construction work by Jefferson's artisan slaves. One of the earliest examples of the classicism in America.

MATHER BROWN, *Portrait of Thomas Jefferson.* 1786. Canvas. Private Collection.

BENJAMIN HENRY LATROBE, *Portrait of Thomas Jefferson.* Pencil drawing. Maryland Historical Society, Baltimore.

JEAN ANTOINE HOUDON, *Statue of George Washington.* 1788-92. Marble, height 74". State Capitol, Richmond, Virginia.

JOHN TRUMBULL, *Battle of Bunker Hill, June 17, 1775.* 1786. Canvas, 25x34". Yale University Art Gallery.

JOHN TRUMBULL, *Death of General Mercer at the Battle of Princeton, January 3, 1777.* 1787-90. Canvas, 20¾x30¾". Yale University Art Gallery.

JOHN TRUMBULL, *Surrender of Lord Cornwallis at Yorktown, October 9, 1781.* 1786-94. Canvas, 21⅛x30⅝". Yale University Art Gallery.

GILBERT STUART, *Portrait of George Washington.* Replica of Stuart's "Athenaeum" type of Washington portraits. (Original painted 1796; 48x37"; Museum of Fine Arts, Boston.) Mount Vernon, Virginia.

Attack on the Bastille, July 14, 1789. 18th century. Print. Musée Carnavalet, Paris.

Mementos of the Bastille. Model made from a stone from the demolished prison. Key to the Bastille presented to Washington by Lafayette. Mount Vernon, Virginia.

Mount Vernon. Home of George Washington from 1747 until his death in 1799. Built by his half-brother Lawrence Washington in 1743 with additions made by George Washington after 1783. Wooden structure of Georgian design; lawns, gardens and subsidiary buildings surround it. It overlooks the Potomac River in Virginia, near Alexandria.

Washington Monument. 1848-85. Height 555'5⅛". Hollow shaft built, in part, after design of Robert Mills. Washington, D.C.

Thomas Jefferson Memorial. Marble monument on the Tidal Basin. Built 1934-43, adapted from plans by John Russell Pope. Washington, D.C.

11. The Worship of Nature

The birth of Romanticism with Jean Jacques Rousseau, Goethe, Wordsworth and Coleridge; of the rediscovery of the beauty of natural landscape by John Constable, and the tremendous achievements of Turner, whose work anticipates generations of painters to come, including the Impressionists.

"For almost a thousand years the chief creative force in western civilisation was Christianity. Then, in about the year 1730, it suddenly declined —in intellectual society practically disappeared. Of course it left a vacuum. People couldn't get on without a belief in something outside themselves, and during the next hundred years they concocted a new belief which, however irrational it may seem to us, has added a good deal to our civilisation—a belief in the divinity of nature."

The worship of nature is a major aspect of the Romantic Movement which began in the later part of the 18th century and flowered in the 19th. Where Classicism demanded the neat, the symmetrical, the orderly and the rational, Romanticism emphasized the emotional, the infinite, the irrational and sometimes the violent and frightening. The shift was largely from the intellect to the emotions and the instincts. It involved not only a new attitude of man toward nature, of which he felt himself almost mystically a part, but also a new concept of man's own nature, as an emotional being, responding to natural stimuli which previous generations had denied. Nature also took on a symbolic character, becoming an expression of the divine, "serene order," in Ralph Waldo Emerson's words, "inviolable by us. It is, therefore, to us, the . . . expositor of the divine mind."

Literature is a major element in the Romantic Movement, as shown by the international popularity of the works of Sir Walter Scott and Lord Byron; and literary qualities invade the other arts. The equation of nature with truth, which Lord Clark points out, brings in a moral element as well. The standard earlier notion of untouched nature as a horrid wilderness to be avoided like the plague gave way to a seeking out of solitude, an enjoyment of wildness for its own sake. This appears not only in the poems of Collins, Wordsworth, Coleridge and others which are quoted in the program, but also appears in the landscapes of Constable and of Turner.

Many of the paintings of George Stubbs (1724-1806) and of the Swiss-born Henry Fuseli (1741-1825) contain a nightmarish quality which resembles the mood of the Gothic novel then in vogue, tales of ghosts, mysterious apparitions, abductions, brigands, dungeons and inexplicable disappearances. Among the most famous of these novels are *The Castle of Otranto* by Horace Walpole, who built himself a sham Gothic country house, Mrs. Radcliffe's *Mysteries of Udolpho,* and *Vathek, An Oriental Tale* by an eccentric millionaire who built an immense pseudo-Gothic pile called Fonthill Abbey, whose battlements he used to stalk at night like the ghost of Hamlet's father.

Edmund Burke's famous essay on "the Sublime and the Beautiful," published in 1756, was important in calling attention to the characteristics of natural landscape, and prepared the way for the concept of the Picturesque, the idea of looking at landscape as one looks at a painting, a notion which persisted throughout much of the 19th century. The naturalistic, as opposed to the formal—and therefore classical—garden, as at Versailles, for example, is another manifestation of this attitude. Always known as the "English Garden," it had a great vogue all over Europe and in America as well.

The Gothic Revival in architecture, pioneered by Horace Walpole at Strawberry Hill, is another important aspect of Romanticism. Charles Barry's Gothic Houses of Parliament (1840-65) in London are an outstanding example. It was because of the Revival that so many 19th-century churches and collegiate buildings were designed in a medieval style. Sir Walter Scott's Abbotsford and the royal country house in Scotland, Balmoral Castle, built by Queen Victoria and Prince Albert are other examples. Alexander Jackson Davis (1803-92) and Richard Upjohn (1802-78) produced distinguished Gothic Revival buildings in America, while Henry Hobson Richardson (1838-86) of the next generation turned another medieval revival style—Romanesque—into a personal style of great power, as shown by his Trinity Church, Boston, and the Marshall Field Warehouse, Chicago. Richardson's achievements led directly into the beginnings of Modernism with Louis Sullivan and others of the Chicago School who created the skyscraper, and provided the proving ground for Frank Lloyd Wright (1869-1959), the Jeffersonian idealist who was the great seminal influence in modern architecture, both in the United States and abroad.

The tendencies toward exoticism inherent in Romanticism, seen in Byron's poetry and other literature, reached eccentric heights in such buildings as the Prince Regent's Royal Pavilion in Brighton (designed by John Nash (1814-21), a wild combination of East Indian and Middle Eastern motives resulting in a picturesque "folly," comparable to Beckford's Fonthill Abbey, though far more amusing. Iranistan, the house in Bridgeport, Connecticut, designed for P. T. Barnum, the circus magnate, by Leopold Eidlitz in 1848 in, if anything, an even more exaggerated Eastern style, was an equally extravagant example of the search for the exotic, and a perfect setting for the man who was perhaps the most uninhibited press agent—a particularly American art form—of modern times.

To find the beginnings of Romanticism in painting, we must return to the late 18th century and the work of two Americans resident in London, Benjamin West and John Singleton Copley. West designed fantastic windows for Beckford's Fonthill Abbey, and, in his *Death of General Wolfe* (1770), for the first time in a major work, clad the participants in that tragic event in the uniforms they actually wore. Further, in the ominous sky and the brooding figure of a seated Indian, he created a deeply expressive mood. His later *Death on a Pale Horse* is a Wagnerian conception. Copley's first major painting, done shortly after he reached London on the eve of the American Revolution, was his *Watson and the Shark* (1778), a dramatic episode involving ordinary people, a frightening and disturbing scene, unresolved, and caught at a crucial moment.

In the meantime, Gavin Hamilton (1723-98) a comparatively unknown British painter, worked in Italy and painted largely classic subjects in a similar mood. Thus the two American colonials shared with a minor British expatriate the honors of producing the prototypes of Romantic painting in Europe.

In France, Théodore Géricault (1791-1824) and Eugène Delacroix (1798-1863) launched Romantic painting with works of great drama, which, because of their propaganda impact, belong to the supplement to the next program. It is interesting to note that not only did Géricault visit England, but the works of such British painters as West and Constable were shown in France, greatly influencing the revelation of a new vision and a new attitude toward nature and toward light and atmosphere.

In Germany, Caspar David Friedrich (1774-1840) represented the Romantic movement by such dramatic scenes as the desolation of ice in his *Wreck of the 'Hope'* (1821, Kunsthalle, Hamburg), while in America Washington Allston (1779-1843) was developing the landscape of mood in which the subject no longer tells a story, as in *Watson and the Shark* or *Raft of the "Medusa,"* but the emotional atmsophere of the picture is its actual subject. His *Moonlit Landscape* (1819, Boston Museum) has mysterious figures and a sailboat drawn up on the shore. It could have been suggested by one of Byron's poems, or one of Allston's own, for that matter. But the real subject is the mood, enigmatic, full of quiet suspense.

Allston was as famous in Europe as in America. He was a friend of Samuel Taylor Coleridge, who wrote critical reviews of Allston's paintings when they were exhibited in England. Curiously, Allston's theories of the emotive effects of color, evolved around the turn of the 19th century, parallel the interpretation by Lord Clark of Turner's paintings. "Titian, Tintoret and Paul Veronese absolutely enchanted me, for they took away all sense of subject. . . . It was the poetry of color which I felt: procreative in its nature, giving birth to a thousand things which the eye cannot see, and distinct from their cause. . . . Now I . . . *think* I understand why so many colorists . . . gave so little heed to the ostensible *stories* of their compositions. . . . They addressed themselves not to the senses merely . . . but rather through them to that region . . . of the imagination . . . supposed to be under the exclusive domination of music, and which, by similar excitement, they caused to teem with visions. . . . In other words they leave the subject to be made by the spectator, provided he possessed the imaginative faculty—otherwise they will have little more meaning for him than a calico counterpane."

The young American studying abroad not only suggests here the function of color in Turner's work, but states a fundamental principle of the experimental art of today, thus showing the Romantic movement to be preparatory to the dramatic developments of more recent years. It is interesting also to note that the feeling of identity with nature which, as Lord Clark points out, was an intense personal experience of Rousseau and others, and which he states in the final program to be a strongly held personal belief, is not only the product of the Romantic movement but also the conviction of increasing numbers of people today who are deeply interested in ecology and worried for the future of life in a polluted and over-industrialized world.

In America a growing awareness of this underlay the rediscovery of the beauty of wild nature in the New World by the painter Thomas Cole (1801-48), the founder of what came to be called the Hudson River School, but which represented actually much more. Cole and such followers as Frederick Church (1826-1900) and John F. Kensett (1818-72) reflected the almost pantheistic view of nature expressed by the philosopher and essayist Ralph Waldo Emerson and the poet William Cullen Bryant, with an acute sense of the passage of time. It was the attitude which led Henry Thoreau to state that "in wildness is the preservation of the world," to the conservation efforts of John Muir to save the giant redwoods on the West Coast, and to the activities of such groups as the Sierra Club today.

America produced only one important Romantic sculptor, William Rimmer (1816-79), a doctor, brilliant anatomist and teacher of drawing, and a painter as well. His life-sized *Falling Gladiator* (bronze, Metropolitan) was the transformation of a life of personal tragedy into a symbol of the national tragedy of the Civil War. When the original plaster was exhibited in the Paris Salon of 1861, critics asked the same question they were to ask of Rodin's *Age of Bronze* fifteen years later: was it cast from a human model? Rimmer's work is an extraordinary anticipation of Rodin in its power and sense of human pathos, expressed through form and gesture.

Fountains Abbey, Yorkshire, northwest England. It was founded in 1137, soon after Rivaulx, the first Cistercian abbey in England. After England became Protestant in the 16th century, it was partially pulled down. The area is famous in English art history as a favorite subject of 19th century water-colorists, including Girtin and Cotman.

THOMAS GAINSBOROUGH, *The Watering Place*. 1777. 58x71". National Gallery, London.

THOMAS GAINSBOROUGH, *The Bridge*. c. 1783. Oil on canvas, 15½ x19". Tate Gallery, London.

THOMAS GAINSBOROUGH, *Mountain Landscape with Peasants Crossing a Bridge*. c. 1787. Oil, 44½x55½". National Gallery of Art, Washington.

JOHN ROBERT COZENS, *Lake of Albano and Castle Gandolfo*. c. 1783-88. Water color, 19¼x26¾". Tate Gallery, London.

ANDRÉ LE NÔTRE, Formal Gardens at Versailles. Late 17th century.

LANCELOT (CAPABILITY) BROWN, English garden or park at Blenheim Palace, Oxfordshire. 18th century.

QUENTIN DE LATOUR, *Jean Jacques Rousseau*. 1753 (?). Pastel, 17⅝ x13⅜". Musée A. Lecuyer, St. Quentin.

LEONARDO DA VINCI, *The Virgin and Child with St. Anne*. 1500. Panel, 5'6⅛"x4'3¼". Louvre, Paris.

PIETER BRUEGEL, *Alpine landscape drawing*. Pen. c. 1555-56. British Museum, London.

PIETER BRUEGEL, *Return of the Herd*. 1565. Panel, 3'10"x5'2⅝". Kunstmuseum, Vienna.

CASPAR WOLF, *Lauteraargletscher*. 1776. Oil. Kunstmuseum, Basle.

ALLAN RAMSAY, *Rousseau in Fur Hat*. c. 1766. Oil on canvas, 29¾ x24⅜". National Gallery of Scotland, Edinburgh.

Rousseau's house near Lac de Bienne, Switzerland.

GEORGE STUBBS, *White Horse Frightened by a Lion*. 1770. Canvas, 40x50¼". Walker Art Gallery, Liverpool.

GEORGE STUBBS, *Lion Attacking a Horse*. c. 1790. National Gallery of Victoria, Melbourne.

WILLIAM HODGES, *The Resolution and Adventure at Tahiti*. 1774. National Maritime Museum, Greenwich, England.

WILLIAM HODGES, *Tahitian Ladies Bathing*. 1773-75. National Maritime Museum, Greenwich, England.

WILLIAM HOGARTH, *Orgy,* from *The Rake's Progress.* 1732-33. Oil, 24½x29½". Sir John Soane's Museum, London.

WILLIAM HODGES, *Tahitian Woman.* 1773-75. National Maritime Museum, Greenwich, England.

WILLIAM HOGARTH, *Chairing the Member,* from *The Election.* 1754. Oil, 40x50". Sir John Soane's Museum, London.

WILLIAM HODGES, *Tahiti Revisited.* 1773. Canvas, 36½x54½". National Maritime Museum, Greenwich, England.

J. H. W. TISCHBEIN, *Goethe in the Campagna.* 1786-87. Canvas, 5'4"x6'7". Städelsches Kunstinstitut, Frankfurt.

JOHANN WOLFGANG VON GOETHE, *Drawings of bones and plants.* Ink. Goethe National Museum, Weimar.

CASPAR DAVID FRIEDRICH, *Morning.* 1820-25. Oil, 8⅝x12". Kunstfreunde, Hanover.

CASPAR DAVID FRIEDRICH, *Man looking at Mountain with Rainbow.* c. 1809. Oil on canvas, 27½x40½". Folkwang Museum, Essen, Germany.

B. R. HAYDON, *Wordsworth Portrait.* c. 1842. Oil, 4'1"x3'6". National Portrait Gallery, London.

Tintern Abbey, western England. Ruins of an abbey founded in 1131 by Cistercians. It is the subject of a poem by Wordsworth and of numerous paintings and etchings by 19th-century English artists.

Lake District, northwest England. Area of lakes and low mountains; the home of Wordsworth and the setting of much of his poetry. Shown here: Rydall Water and Wordsworth's cottage at Grasmere.

Dorothy Wordsworth. Oil portrait.

J. M. W. TURNER, *Buttermere Lake with Rainbow.* 1797. Oil on canvas, 35x47". Tate Gallery, London.

J. M. W. TURNER, *Frosty Morning.* 1813. Oil on canvas, 44¾x68¾". Tate Gallery, London.

JOHN CONSTABLE, *The Cornfield.* 1826. Canvas, 56¼x48". National Gallery, London.

JOHN CONSTABLE, *Tree Studies,* among them: No. 234. c. 1821? Oil on paper, 9¾x11½". Victoria and Albert Museum, London.

JOHN CONSTABLE, *The Haywain.* 1821. Canvas, 51¼x73". National Gallery, London.

JOHN CONSTABLE, *Dedham Lock and Mill.* 1820. Oil on canvas, 21⅛x 30". Victoria and Albert Museum, London.

JOHN CONSTABLE, *Stoke-by-Nayland, Suffolk.* c. 1830. Oil on canvas, 7x10". Tate Gallery, London.

JOHN CONSTABLE, *Cottage in a Cornfield*. 1833. Oil on canvas, 24½ x 20¼ ". Victoria and Albert Museum, London.

JOHN CONSTABLE, *Willows by a Stream near Salisbury*. 1829. Oil on canvas, 18x21¾ ". Victoria and Albert Museum, London.

JOHN CONSTABLE, *The Leaping Horse*. 1825. Oil on canvas, 53½ x71". Royal Academy, London.

JOHN CONSTABLE, *Barges on the Stour*. 1811. Oil on paper laid on canvas, 10¼ x12¼ ". Victoria and Albert Museum, London.

JOHN CONSTABLE, *Sketch for Dedham Mill*. c. 1810-15. Oil on paper, 7⅛ x9¾ ". Victoria and Albert Museum, London.

JOHN CONSTABLE, *Flatford Mill from a Lock on the Stour*. c. 1811? Oil on canvas, 9¾ x11¾ ". Victoria and Albert Museum, London.

JOHN CONSTABLE, *Spring Ploughing*. c. 1809-16. Oil on panel, 7½ x 14¼ ". Victoria and Albert Museum, London.

JOHN CONSTABLE, *Study for Branch Hill Pond, Hampstead Heath*. 1819. Oil on canvas, 10x11⅞". Victoria and Albert Museum, London.

J. M. W. TURNER, *Chamonix and Mer de Glace*. 1803/4. Watercolor. Mellon Collection, Upperville, Virginia.

J. M. W. TURNER, *Avalanche in the Grisons*. 1810. Oil on canvas, 35½ x47¼ ". Tate Gallery, London.

J. M. W. TURNER, *Snowstorm on Mount Cenis*. 1820. Watercolor. Private Collection (Mrs. Dorian Williamson), London.

J. M. W. TURNER, *Snowstorm: Hannibal Crossing the Alps*. 1812. Oil, 57x93". Tate Gallery, London.

J. M. W. TURNER, *Valley of Aosta—Snowstorm*. c. 1836/37. Oil on canvas, 36x48¼ ". Art Institute, Chicago.

J. M. W. TURNER, *The Parting of Hero and Leander*. 1837. Oil on canvas, 57½ x93". National Gallery, London.

J. M. W. TURNER, *Rocky Bay with Figures*. c. 1828-30. Oil on canvas, 35½ x48½ ". Tate Gallery, London.

J. M. W. TURNER, *Fighting Temeraire*. 1839. Canvas, 35¾ x48". National Gallery, London.

J. M. W. TURNER, *Regatta at Cowes*. Oil on canvas, 18x24". Tate Gallery, London.

J. M. W. TURNER, *Interior at Petworth*. 1837. Oil on canvas, 35¾ x 48". Tate Gallery, London.

J. M. W. TURNER, *Ladies at Piano at Petworth* or *Music at Petworth*. c. 1833. Oil, 48x35½ ". Tate Gallery, London.

J. M. W. TURNER, *Rain, Steam and Speed*. 1844. Oil on canvas, 35¾ x

48". National Gallery, London.

J. M. W. TURNER, *Landscape with Cattle and Cow, Norham Castle, Sunrise.* c. 1835-40. Oil on canvas, 35¾x48". Tate Gallery, London.

J. M. W. TURNER, *Yacht Approaching the Coast.* c. 1835-40. Oil on canvas, 40¼x56". Tate Gallery, London.

J. M. W. TURNER, *Sunrise with Boats between Headlands.* c. 1835-40. Oil on canvas, 36x48". Tate Gallery, London.

JOHN RUSKIN, *Study of Gneiss Rock.* Ink. Ashmolean Museum, Oxford.

JOHN RUSKIN, *Candytuft drawing.* Ink. Ruskin Gallery, Isle of Wight.

JOHN RUSKIN, *Thistle drawing.* Ink. Ruskin Gallery, Isle of Wight.

JOHN RUSKIN, *Tree Avenue.* Black and sepia ink. Ruskin Gallery, Isle of Wight.

JOHN RUSKIN, *Study of Dawn.* Watercolor. Ashmolean Museum, Oxford.

JOHN CONSTABLE, *Cloud studies,* among them No. 328. 1830. Watercolor, 9x7½". Victoria and Albert Museum, London.

J. M. W. TURNER, *Slave Ship.* 1840. Oil, 2' 11¾"x4'. Boston Museum of Fine Arts.

J. M. W. TURNER, *The Evening Star.* c. 1830-40. Canvas, 3'¼"x4'¼". National Gallery, London.

J. M. W. TURNER, Montage of seascapes from the Tate Gallery, among them *Waves Breaking on a Lee Shore.* c. 1835. Oil on canvas, 18¼x 23¾". Tate Gallery, London.

JACKSON POLLOCK, *One. 1950* Oil. Staatgalerie, Stuttgart.

PIERRE AUGUSTE RENOIR, *La Grenouillère.* 1868-9. Oil. 25¾x31½". National Museum, Stockholm.

EDOUARD MANET, *Monet Painting in His Floating Studio.* 1874. Oil on canvas, 32¼x39⅜". Neue Pinakothek, Munich.

CLAUDE MONET, *La Grenouillère.* 1869. Oil on canvas, 29⅜x39¼". Metropolitan Museum of Art, New York.

CLAUDE MONET, *The Bridge at Argenteuil.* 1874. Oil on canvas, 23⅝x 31½". Louvre, Paris.

PIERRE RENOIR, *A Path Rising in High Grass.* 1876-8. Canvas. Jeu de Paume, Paris.

GEORGES SEURAT, *Bridge of Courbevoie.* 1886. Canvas, 18x21½". Courtauld Institute Gallery, London.

CLAUDE MONET, *Regatta at Argenteuil.* 1874. Oil, 23½x38¾". Louvre, Paris.

CLAUDE MONET, *Waterlilies.* c. 1919-26. Oil on canvas. Musée de l'Orangerie, Paris.

12. The Fallacies of Hope

The Age of Reason gives way to the Age of Revolution, of violence and anarchy, succeeded in turn by the Napoleonic empire; both the hopes and the despair were expressed in the music of Beethoven and the painting of Goya, first and greatest of the artists committed to be mankind's conscience; the paintings of protest of Géricault and Delacroix, given force by the feelings let loose by Romanticism; Daumier and his compassion for man, and Rodin as the last great Romantic artist, who gave final expression to Romantic man's tragic destiny.

"With the appearance of General Bonaparte the liberated energies of the Revolution take a new direction—the insatiable urge to conquer and explore. But what has this to do with civilisation? War and Imperialism, so long the most admired of human activities, have fallen into disrepute, and I am enough a child of my time to hate them both. But I recognise that together with much that is destructive, they are symptoms of a life-giving impulse. 'And shall I die and this unconquered?' The words that Marlowe put into the mouth of the dying Tamerlane could have been spoken by how many of the great poets, artists and scientists. In the field of political action they have become odious to us. But I have an uneasy feeling that we cannot have one without the other. Ruskin's unwelcome words 'no great art ever yet rose on earth but among a nation of soldiers' seem to me historically irrefutable—so far."

In this program, Lord Clark considers Revolution, especially the French Revolution, as an aspect of Romanticism, in that it was an expression in extreme degree of the new sense of individualism and of individual freedom engendered by the Romantic movement. Painters have acted as propagandists from early times, the Baroque artists of the Counter Reformation were propagandists for Catholic orthodoxy, just as the artists working for Louis XIV of France devoted their skills to propagandizing the idea of the absolute monarch ruling through God's will.

Jacques Louis David (1748-1825), who was mentioned in connection with the 10th program, was chief propagandist of the French Revolution, and after the advent of Napoleon, as enthusiastic a proponent of the Empire as he had been of the Revolution earlier. In the fullness of realization of his canvasses, with their richness of detail, he shows an interpretation obviously favorable to the ideology involved in each case. David's successor, Ingres (1780-1867), also mentioned in connection with the 10th program, was often another propagandist for the imperial ideal.

97

Where David and Ingres were strict Poussinists, Théodore Géricault (1791-1824) and Eugène Delacroix (1798-1863) were equally definitely in the Rubenist tradition. Géricault's vast canvas, *Raft of the "Medusa"* (1818-19), of which Lord Clark gives the background, is Romantic painting at its most intense, with its starving, dead and dying survivors of a tragedy at sea which was the result of official incompetence and criminal irresponsibility. The tendencies toward violence which seem to be often a part of Romanticism—the violence of man reflecting the superhuman violence of nature suggested in Copley's *Watson and the Shark* mentioned earlier—appear in such paintings as this and many other of Géricault's works. Yet Romanticism's intense interest in human personality and emotional and inner life led Géricault to become a friend of Dr. Georget, one of the founders of psychiatry, and to paint objective but clearly sympathetic portraits of various inmates of the asylum where the doctor did much of his work.

Like so many Romantic figures, Géricault died comparatively young, leaving his near contemporary, Eugène Delacroix, to dominate the field of painting in the Rubenist tradition. His *Massacre at Chios*, first exhibited in Paris in 1824, instantly established his position. For years he and Ingres, representing the opposing tradition of David, were deadly rivals. Delacroix's *Massacre* was as clearly propagandistic as Géricault's *Raft*. It reflected the universal sympathy with the struggle of the Greeks for independence from the Turks, the cause for which Byron died, and for which President Monroe was urged by a member of his cabinet to send the assistance of the American fleet. Delacroix also satisfied the Romantic taste for the exotic by his colorful harem scenes and voluptuous odalisques, anticipating by more than half a century a favorite theme of Matisse.

Though both Géricault and Delacroix expressed in their art their disgust at human cruelty, an earlier artist, contemporary with David, gave the most passionate and unrelenting expression to his horror of man's inhumanity to man: the great Spaniard, Francisco Goya (1746-1828). In any account of the turn of the arts to protest, which was an important aspect of the Romantic movement, Goya's name must head the list. The greatest artist of his era, his work transcends his time. The series of etchings, *The Disasters of War*, contain perhaps the most telling works of art of their kind ever produced, combining an intense and sensitive human sympathy with the incredible brutality which characterized the Spanish civil war and French invasion.

Goya's painted cartoons for tapestries to be woven in the royal factory are of carefree scenes rendered in tones of Rococo lightness, yet in later works, when, as with Beethoven, deafness increased his solitariness, he painted a series of black paintings which are nightmare visions of overwhelming horror. Throughout his vividly productive career, his gigantic individualism towers above the rest of the artists of his period, as does his hatred of hypocrisy; underlying all, his intense human sympathy. As was the case with so many of the great Romantics, his humanism was even greater than his pessimism. He is the ancestor of all the many artists since his time who have acted as man's conscience in their stand against war and its cruelties, all the way down to our times when the same Spanish fierceness reappears in Picasso's *Guernica* (1937), painted to protest the violence of another, more recent Spanish civil war.

Though his works were on a smaller scale—many of them lithographs produced in popular periodicals—Honoré Daumier (1808-79), painter, printmaker and sculptor, was also totally committed to the cause of humanity and created some of its most compelling statements. In series of caricatures he revealed the pretentiousness of the bourgeoisie—the product of the developing industrial revolution—of their overfed, self-satisfied way of life, of their disregard for the grinding poverty which increasing industralization produced. He satirized the venality and corruption of lawyers and judges. His small sculptured busts of members of parliament and officers of state are devastating caricatures of human greed, vanity, selfishness, and stupidity. But in such paintings as *The Uprising,* (Phillips Collection, Washington, D. C.), illustrated on the program, *The Third-Class Carriage* (Metropolitan, New York) and the several small paintings of washerwomen, he reveals the depth of his own humanity. And in the expressiveness of brushwork in his paintings and of form in his sculptures he reveals himself almong the ancestors of modern art.

The theme of Don Quixote, of a grotesque but somehow noble representative of the virtues of an earlier and less sophisticated society, appealed to Daumier who painted subjects from Cervantes' famous novel often. The most famous illustrator of the period, however, was Gustave Doré (1832-83), whose work is shown several times in these programs. Influenced by the far greater Daumier,

Doré painted colossal theatrical canvasses with romantic story-telling subjects, now utterly forgotten. As a romantic illustrator, however, he displays more lasting qualities.

Lord Clark's ending of the program with the works of Auguste Rodin (1840-1917) as "the last great romantic artist" is entirely appropriate for the theme of *The Fallacies of Hope*. But Rodin was actually more than that. With the painter Paul Cézanne (1839-1906), he bridged two worlds of art, a destiny he was aware of. The greatest sculptor since Bernini, he returned to the classical past, but even more to the Middle Ages, to try to recall sculpture from the dry and trivial academicism into which it had fallen, and make it an expression of life. He deliberately allowed a piece to evolve as he worked on it, thus giving it a life of its own and an often enigmatic quality which involves the observer. He was the first to exhibit an incomplete figure as a complete work of art, his deeply impressive *Walking Man*, who, because he is headless, becomes, somehow, everyman. He sought to reveal through form and gesture the intense and overwhelmingly inner life of man which the new science of Freudian psychology was beginning to investigate. In all these aspects he anticipates vital qualities of modern art. And as if instinctively aware of the events which were to come—a period of war, revolution and destruction—his greatest figures, except for the heroic Balzac and his distinguished portrait busts, are in the grip of passion and despair; intensely human and thus intensely moving, they seem overwhelmed by tragedy.

Works of art as they appear in Program 12

AUGUSTE RODIN, *The Gates of Hell*. Bronze. Height 21', width 8'. Rodin Museum, Paris. Commissioned by the French government in 1880 for the Musée des Arts Décoratifs. A version was completed in 1900, but Rodin never considered it finished. Many figures on the door were cast as separate, larger pieces, such as *The Thinker*.

Osterly Park House, Middlesex, England. Built c. 1575, remodelled 1761-80 by Robert and James Adam. Shown: library, hall and exterior.

PIERRE ANTOINE DEMACHY, *Celebrations of National Unity, Place de la Concorde, Paris*. Late 18th century. Canvas. Musée Carnavalet, Paris.

Lafayette Taking the Oath of the Constitution. Late 18th century.

Canvas. Musée Carnavalet, Paris.

The French Revolutionary Camille Desmoulins Haranguing a Crowd. Late 18th century. Print.

Entrance to the Chamber of Deputies, Paris. Late 18th century. Print.

JACQUES LOUIS DAVID, *The Oath of the Tennis Court.* 1791. Wash drawing, study for a painting never completed. Versailles.

Crowds Marching into Cannon; Women Marching into Pikes. Late 18th century. Prints.

FRANÇOIS RUDE, *La Marseillaise; or Departure of the Volunteers in 1792.* 1833-36. 42x26'. Arc de Triomphe, Paris. Soldiers shown in guise of ancient Gauls. Above them, a winged Victory in classical garb.

Arc de Triomphe, Paris. 1806-36. Triumphal arch built after the plans of the architect Jean François Chalgrin (1739-1811) to honor the glory of Napoleon's imperial armies. Place de l'Etoile, Paris.

LOUIS LEOPOLD BOILLY, *Triumph of Marat.* c. 1793. Canvas.

Detail of crowd. Late 18th century. Print.

Champs de Mars, 14th of July. Late 18th century. Print.

Revolutionary Months. Late 18th century. Print. Shown: *Ventose, Thermidor, Brumaire.*

JACQUES LOUIS DAVID, *Madame Verminac.* 1799. Canvas, 56¼ x 43¼". Louvre, Paris.

JACQUES LOUIS DAVID, *Madame Récamier.* 1800. Canvas, 5'6⅞"x 7'10½". Louvre, Paris.

Demolition of the Eglise de Feuillant. Late 18th century. Canvas. Musée Carnavalet, Paris.

HUBERT ROBERT, *Demolition of the Church of St. Jean-en-Grève.* 1800. Canvas, 24½ x21". Musée Carnavalet, Paris.

PIERRE ANTOINE DEMACHY, *The Celebration of the Supreme Being.* Late 18th century. Canvas. Musée Carnavalet, Paris.

JEAN BAPTISTE MALLET, *The Cult of Nature.* Late 18th century. Bibliothèque Nationale, Paris.

HUBERT ROBERT, *Interior of the Prison of St. Lazare.* 1793. Canvas, 15½ x12½". Musée Carnavalet.

Guillotine in the Place du Carrousel. Late 18th century. Print.

JEAN BAPTISTE MALLET, *Departure for the Guillotine.* Late 18th century. Musée Carnavalet, Paris.

Massacre of September, 1792. Late 18th century. Print.

Basket of Heads. Late 18th century. Printed caricature.

The Committee. Late 18th century. Print.

Massacre of September, 1792, at St. Germain des Près (details). The massacre of prisoners took place at the corner of the present Rue de l'Abbaye and Rue Bonaparte, September 2-4, 1792. Late 18th century. Prints.

Declaration of Rights (detail). Late 18th century. Print.

Arrest of Robespierre, July 27, 1794. Late 18th century. Print.

Guillotining of Robespierre, July 28, 1794. Late 18th century. Print.

JACQUES LOUIS DAVID, *The Death of Marat.* 1793. Canvas, 65x50½". Royal Museum of Fine Arts, Brussels.

JACQUES LOUIS DAVID, *La Maraîchère.* 1795. Paper on canvas, 32x25". Musée des Beaux Arts, Lyons.

PIERRE ANTOINE DEMACHY, *Crowd around Guillotine.* Late 18th century. Canvas. Musée Carnavalet, Paris.

HENRI FELIX EMMANUEL PHILIPPOTEAUX, *Napoleon at Rivoli, January 14, 1797.* c. mid-19th century. Canvas. Versailles.

Malmaison. Château at Rueil-Malmaison, suburb of Paris, home of Napoleon and Josephine, 1800-3, and of Josephine after the divorce from Napoleon (1809-14). Built in the 17th century, it was enlarged and embellished by the architects Charles Percier (1764-1838) and Pierre F. L. Fontaine (1762-1883) for Josephine. Shown: Napoleon's council chamber, with ceiling made to look like a tent, and Napoleon's library and study. The château is now an art and history museum of the Napoleonic Era.

BARON ANTOINE JEAN GROS, *Napoleon at Arcole.* 1796. Canvas, 28⅜x23¼". Louvre, Paris.

BARON ANTOINE JEAN GROS, *Napoleon as First Consul.* 1802. Canvas. Musée de la Légion d'Honneur, Paris.

JEAN AUGUSTE DOMINIQUE INGRES, *Napoleon as Emperor.* 1806. Canvas, 8'6⅝"x5'3". Musée de l'Armée, Paris.

JACQUES LOUIS DAVID, *Napoleon Crossing Great St. Bernard Pass in the Alps.* 1800. Canvas, 8'1"x7'7". Versailles (one of four versions).

ANNE LOUIS GIRODET-TRIOSON, *Ossian Playing the Harp.* c. 1801. Canvas. Malmaison.

JEAN AUGUSTE DOMINIQUE INGRES, *Dream of Ossian.* 1813. Canvas, 11'5"x9'. Ingres Museum, Montauban.

ANNE LOUIS GIRODET-TRIOSON, *Ossian Receiving Napoleon's Marshalls in Valhalla.* c. 1801. Canvas. Malmaison.

JACQUES LOUIS DAVID, *Distribution of the Eagles on the 5th December, 1804.* 1810. Canvas. 20x30'6". Versailles.

Tomb of Napoleon, Church of Les Invalides, Paris. Begun 1843 after the design of Visconti, a 19th-century architect; set in a circular crypt under the dome of the church. Around tomb is a circular gallery with 12 huge figures of Victory by James Pradier and ten bas reliefs by Charles Simart depicting the great success of Napoleon.

HUBERT ROBERT, *Destruction of the Bastille, 1789.* 1789. Canvas, 30⅜x45″. Musée Carnavalet.

Vincennes. Outside of Paris. A royal residence since the 12th century with huge castle that dates in part from the 14th century. The dungeon became a state prison in the 17th century. Diderot was one of many political prisoners held there; in 1944 French hostages were killed there by the Germans.

Revolution of 1830, Paris. 19th century. Print.

Revolution of 1848, Spain: Fighting at the Barricades in Cadiz. Mid-19th century. Print.

Revolution of 1848, Berlin: Conflict in front of the Royal Palace. Mid-19th century. Print.

Revolution of 1848, Paris: Barricades at a corner of the Rue Mazarine. Mid-19th century. Print.

Revolution of 1848, Hungary: Riots in front of the Opera House, Budapest. Mid-19th century. Print.

Italy, 1861: A Man Lying Dead. 1861. Photograph.

France, 1871: Man being shot by a firing squad. 19th century. Print.

Russian Revolution, 1917: Shooting on troops, crowds running, Petrograd. 1917. Film.

Spanish Civil War, 1936: Crowds and explosion. 1936. Film.

Revolution in Hungary, 1956: burning flag, shattering of Stalin's statue, carrying stretchers. Film.

Revolution in France, 1968: French students march carrying banners. 1968. Film.

FRANCISCO GOYA, *The Third of May, 1808.* 1814-15. Canvas, 8′9″x 13′4″. Depicts the shooting of Spanish liberals by the troops of Napoleon. The Prado, Madrid.

Portrait of Byron. Private Collection.

Portrait of Byron. 19th century. Canvas. National Portrait Gallery, London.

Byron Standing by a Lake. 19th century. Print.

Castle of Chillon. At the eastern end of the Lake of Geneva. Built between the 9th and the 13th centuries, residence of the counts of Savoy. François de Bonnivard, supporter of revolt of Genève against Charles III of Savoy, was imprisoned there from 1530-1536. He was the original prisoner of Chillon romanticized in Byron's poem.

J. M. W. TURNER, *Fire at Sea*. c. 1835. Canvas, 67½x86¾". Tate Gallery, London.

J. M. W. TURNER, *The Slave Ship*. 1839. Canvas, 35¾x48". Museum of Fine Arts, Boston.

THÉODORE GÉRICAULT, *The Raft of the "Medusa."* 1818-19. Canvas, 16'1"x23'6". Louvre, Paris.

THÉODORE GÉRICAULT, Preliminary version *The Raft of the "Medusa."* Canvas, 25⅝x32¾". Louvre, Paris.

THÉODORE GÉRICAULT, *Head of drowned man*. 1818? Canvas, 14½x 12". Geneva, Musée d'Art et d'Histoire.

THÉODORE GÉRICAULT, *Man guillotined*. 1818. Canvas, 18x22". The Art Institute, Chicago.

THÉODORE GÉRICAULT, *The Madman*. 1821-24. Canvas, 24x20". Museum of Fine Arts, Ghent.

THÉODORE GÉRICAULT, *The Madwoman*. 1822-23. Canvas, 30½x 25¼". Louvre, Paris.

THÉODORE GÉRICAULT, *The Madwoman*. 1822-23. Canvas, 28½x 23". Musée, Lyons.

THÉODORE GÉRICAULT, *Self-Portrait*. Canvas. Louvre, Paris.

EUGENÈ DELACROIX, *Self-Portrait*. 1835-37. Canvas, 25¼x20⅛". Louvre, Paris.

EUGENÈ DELACROIX, *Prisoner of Chillon*. 1834. Canvas, 29x36". Louvre, Paris.

EUGENÈ DELACROIX, *The Massacre at Chios*. 1822-24. Canvas, 13'10" x11'7". Louvre, Paris.

EUGENÈ DELACROIX, *Attila Tramples Italy and the Arts*. 1838-47. Oil and wax, 24'1"x36'2". Hemicycle in the Library, Palais Bourbon, Paris.

AUGUSTE RODIN, *Eve*. Bronze, small (original plaster, 1881). Collection of Kenneth Clark, Saltwood Castle.

AUGUSTE RODIN, *Burghers of Calais*. 1884-89; finished work erected in Calais, 1895. Plaster cast. Rodin Museum, Meudon.

HONORÉ DAUMIER, *The Agitator*. Phillips Collection, Washington.

HONORÉ, DAUMIER, *Between the Acts*. Basel.

HONORÉ DAUMIER, *Lawyers*. Private Collection.

GUSTAVE DORÉ, Caricature of theatre audience. 19th century. Print. Details of group of seated men and man with a lorgnette.

GUSTAVE DORÉ, Caricature of a saloon crowd. 19th century. Print.

EUGENÈ DELACROIX, *Self-Portrait*. Mesdag Museum, The Hague.

AUGUSTE RODIN, *Balzac*. 1892-97. Shown are final version (bronze), and studies (plaster), over lifesize. Rodin Museum, Meudon.

13. Heroic Materialism

The industrial revolution and the suffering of the poor; heroic achievements of technology and engineering, and the increasing dehumanization of man; the realism of Courbet with his paintings of peasants, and the deeply committed art of van Gogh; the rise of science creates a new and frightening age and raises the question of the future of man.

"Dorothy Wordworth said about the view from Westminster Bridge that 'it was like one of Nature's own grand spectacles.' Well, nature is violent and brutal, and there's nothing we can do about it. But New York, after all, was made by men. It took almost the same time to reach its present condition as it did to complete the Gothic cathedrals. At which point a very obvious reflection crosses one's mind; that the cathedrals were built to the glory of God, New York was built to the glory of mammon; money, gain, the new god of the nineteenth century."

During the later eighteenth century the reform movement grew in England along with the industrial revolution which was encouraged by the heavy production necessitated by the Napoleonic Wars. It was a parallel development to that which took place in the United States when the Civil War transformed an agricultural and trading nation into a heavily industrialized one. There was the same problem of the desperate lot of the workers, the exploitation of child labor and all the other ills attendant upon uncontrolled and competitive greed.

In England, as America, there were humanitarians like William Wilberforce (1759-1833) to devote their lives to the eradication of the slave trade. England had abolished it by 1811 and France four years later. Spain and Portugal were reluctantly forced by England's example and pressure to do the same shortly afterward. Despite the attempts of the New England abolitionists and the opinions of such leading thinkers as Jefferson, emancipation was not proclaimed until a half century later in the United States.

More than perhaps any other single individual, the English novelist, Charles Dickens (1812-70), in his touching, dramatic and often sentimental accounts of the dreadful conditions of the British poor, helped to promote legislation to improve their lot. It is of interest to note that when Dickens visited Boston in 1842, he stated that "the public institutions and charities of this capital of Massachusetts are as nearly perfect, as the most considerate wisdom, benevolence and humanity can make them." So the same forces were at work on this side of the Atlantic. The architect Charles Bulfinch (1763-1844) pioneered in improved and humanitarian prison design, and his Massachusetts General Hospital Building, begun in 1818, was a model of its kind. Dickens also was delighted with the living and working conditions and the degree of culture of the girls working in American mills. Mill design and workers' housing are often forgotten, though important aspects of American 19th-century architecture. Despite neglect, examples still remain in Manchester, New Hampshire, and in Lowell, Massachusetts. As competition grew, conditions worsened, and the dehumanization of the worker increased—a situation which now pervades almost all aspects of life, including the arts.

The new concept of space which came with the development of railroads, as Lord Clark points out, also involved a new concept of time, and represents another step along the road begun with the development in the Renaissance of the science of perspective, and leading on into the age of space. Also the dramatic achievements in engineering in England, several of which are illustrated in the program, were paralleled in America, with its pioneering tendencies toward the pragmatic solution of problems. There was in the development of the American axe, so much more versatile than its European ancestor, which, with the Kentucky rifle—both the products of German smiths on the Pennsylvania frontier—made possible the conquest of a continent. The indestructable Conestoga wagon which carried families westward was another Pennsylvania invention, while its descendant, the Concord coach, proved its practical ruggedness over the years. The invention, probably in 1833, by a builder-architect named Augustus Deodat Taylor, of the form of construction known, because of the speed with which it made it possible to build as the balloon frame, was another revolutionary step. It was based on the machine production of nails, which had been earlier developed in the United States, and the standardization of lumber sizes based on the 2″ x 4″, made possible as a result of the early perfection of sawmills in America in Colonial days. Following the new method, a man and a boy, with no more tools than a saw and hammer could frame a small house in a few days. This method made possible the extraordinary speed with which new cities grew up and Chicago and San Francisco were rebuilt after disasters.

The use of cast iron in construction was another pioneering architectural and engineering development. In 1830 a bank in Pottsville, Pennsylvania, had a fire-proof cast-iron front, while before mid-century entire buildings were made of this new construction. Both these methods led directly to the dramatic architecture of the present century.

It was in 1850 that the American sculptor living in Florence, Horatio Greenough (1805-52), first suggested that a new aesthetic concept was involved when he defined beauty as "the promise of function," and recognized the clipper ship—the invention of Donald McKay—and the trotting wagon as works of art. In this he foretold the soaring grandeur of modern bridges and skyscrapers, and a new and creative combination of the arts and sciences which is of such importance today.

The Great International Exhibition of 1851 in London, the brainchild of Prince Albert, well illustrates the confusion which existed in mid-19th century as a result of the lack of recognition of the radical change in standards of judgment regarding the arts perceived by Greenough. The displays in Paxton's Crystal Palace were a fascinating, often nightmarish, conglomeration of miscellaneous objects such as a buffet of fantastic and grotesque elaboration made entirely of gutta-percha. But an early model of Samuel Colt's patented revolving pistol was also included, and *The Greek Slave*, a life-size marble nude by the American Hiram Powers (1805-73) was among the hits of the show. Because a group of Cincinnati clergymen had pronounced her "clothed in her own virtue", she combined morality with nudity, and thus was ensured of universal popularity. More important than anything in it was the extraordinary structure of the Palace itself. Using prefabricated parts based on a modular system, Paxton enclosed a maximum of open space with a minimum of structure, thus anticipating several lines of later architectural development.

Just as Charles Dicken's popular novels were propaganda for reform of the life of the poor in England, and Harriet Beecher Stowe's *Uncle Tom's Cabin* was an anti-slavery tract of the greatest power, there were painters who were equally impassioned in their dedication to humanitarianism. Among the most important were the Frenchman Gustave Courbet (1819-77) and Jean François Millet

(1814-75), founder of the Barbizon School. The latter was a follower of Daumier, yet he tended to sentimentalize his peasants and workers in a manner which made them more acceptable to a bourgeois public because it did not directly assault their conscience. Courbet, a big, muscular, bearded radical, had no such scruples. A dedicated socialist, Courbet practiced what he called realism, painting road-menders breaking stones with hammers (1849, destroyed 1945)— a far cry from classical heroes—and a peasant *Funeral at Ornans* (1850, Louvre), illustrating with great dignity his thesis that the only proper, democratic subjects for art were scenes from the everyday lives of peasants and workers.

Edouard Manet (1832-83) came of a wealthy family which dis-approved of his taking up an artistic career. His *Déjeuner sur l'Herbe* (1863) must not have pleased his relatives any more than his famous *Olympia* (1865). The first, based on a composition by Raphael, shows two couples on a picnic in which the young ladies are most unashamedly nude, while the latter is a reclining nude of a young courtesan. Like Courbet, he reflected the strong trend toward realism represented in contemporary literature by his friend, the novelist Emile Zola. Manet often showed his work with the Impressionists Claude Monet (1840-1926) and Pierre Auguste Renoir (1841-1919) in the Salon des Refusés, the exhibition for those whose works were turned down by the conservative, academic juries which ruled the annual official Salon. Impressionism as a movement did not last long. Theoretically, it meant painting the momentary appearance of things seen through atmosphere under the light of a certain time of day. Monet alone continued most consistently in this vein. But it was a movement of great influence, lightening colors and emphasizing a tendency toward momentary, snapshot-like compositions.

But in the meantime a stubborn, independent, morose character appeared upon the scene, Paul Cézanne (1839-1906), who deter-mined to return painting to the classical tradition of Poussin, reduc-ing landscapes, portraits and still lifes alike to the basic forms of the cylinder, the cone and the sphere. He used carefully modulated color to enhance the formal qualities of his work, and developed a type of brushwork which increased the structural emphasis he sought. The results were both impressive and revolutionary. His emphasis on form led on to the Cubist experiments of Picasso and Braque in the early years of this century.

While Georges Seurat (1859-91) took Impressionism over into

a further breaking up of color called Pointillism, with which he produced such fascinating pictures as *Sunday Afternoon on the Island of the Grand Jatte* (1886, The Art Institute, Chicago), Vincent van Gogh (1853-90) and Paul Gauguin (1844-1903) sought different directions. Van Gogh's early work was deeply socially conscious and identified with the plight of the poor. Gradually he developed a personal style, a moving expressionism with patterned brushwork and often brilliant color, suggesting a unity with nature which he sought perhaps unconsciously to counteract his increasingly disturbed mental state which led eventually to insanity and suicide. Yet his paintings are marvelously affirmative statements, sensitively yet boldly expressed. Gauguin's troubled career eventually led him to the South Seas where he painted the richly colored canvasses of native life which gave him fame.

Edgar Degas (1834-1917) was a draftsman in the tradition of Ingres who developed a style in oil and pastel of individual color and carefully calculated compositions, perhaps influenced, like those of the American expatriate, James Whistler (1834-1903), by Japanese prints. The brilliant dwarf, Henri de Toulouse-Lautrec (1864-1901), was a great admirer of Degas, and recorded his coolly objective observations of the low life of Paris, the dance halls and brothels, where he seemed most at home because there he was accepted despite his pitiful deformity.

Henri Matisse (1869-1954) was one of the leading Post-Impressionists who developed a joyously colorful style, based on boldly simplified compositions and a sure and personal undulating line, which he continued through a long and fruitful career. Meanwhile a contemporary, the Russian-born Wassily Kandinsky (1866-1944), was experimenting along highly original lines at the same time that Picasso and Braque were developing Cubism. Influenced by his love of music, Kandinsky sought, according to theories expressed years earlier by the young Washington Allston (see supplement to program 11), to use color expressively but with purely geometric or non-objective forms. This direction and that of Cubism were to lead on to the wide diversity of experiment in the arts of our own times.

The United States was little involved with these European developments, though such American painters as Marsden Hartley (1877-1943) and John Marin (1870-1953) and the sculptor Robert Laurent (1890-1970) were independently experimenting with abstract art during the same years. But America had produced three giants in the later 19th and early 20th centuries: Winslow Homer (1836-1910), whose later work records the epic of man and nature in the New World in terms of Atlantic coast fishermen and Adirondack guides; Thomas Eakins (1844-1916) whose mastery of means and powerful insight are shown by his *Gross Clinic* (1875, Jefferson Medical College, Philadelphia) and his many portraits; and Albert Pinkham Ryder (1847-1917), a husky, gentle recluse of a sea-faring family, who painted such unforgettable visions out of the depths of his imagination as his famous *Toilers of the Sea* (Metropolitan, New York), a solitary boat by moonlight, or *The Dead Bird* (Phillips Collection, Washington).

In Maurice Prendergast (1859-1924) America produced another independent artist with a unique vision. Yet it was not till the famous Armory Show of 1913 that Americans in general became suddenly and shockingly aware of all that had been going on in the European world of art—the experiments of Cubism, Dada, Expressionism and all the rest. That date ushered the United States summarily into the 20th century, with all its restless variety, endless experiment and broad spectrum of styles, from illustrative realism to the happening —all an expression of those forces which make up the modern world and which Lord Clark, like so many of the rest of us, finds so profoundly disturbing.

Works of art as they appear in Program 13

Montage of scenes of New York City. Aerial view of New York. Brooklyn Bridge, John A. Roebling, 1883; the first suspension bridge to use steel-wire cables. George Washington Bridge, Othman H. Ammann, 1931. Statue of Liberty, F. A. Bartholdi, 1884; 152 feet high, constructed of copper sheets. Skater in Central Park. Manhattan skyline from Staten Island Ferry. Pan American Building, Walter Gropius and Emery Roth and Sons, 1963. Central Park surrounded by apartment buildings; the 840-acre park was planned by Calvert Vaux and Frederick Law Olmsted, 1858.

W. PICKETT after PHILIPPE JACQUES DE LOUTHERBOURG, *Iron Works at Coalbrookdale*. 1805. Aquatint. Collection Sir Arthur Elton.

J. M. W. TURNER, *Limekiln at Coalbrookdale*. 1830-40. Canvas. Collection Sir Arthur Elton, Huntingdonshire, England.

Prisoners on a Treadmill. 18th century. Print.

B. READING, *Slaves on African Quayside*. Walker Art Gallery, Liverpool.

JOHN RISING, *Portrait of William Wilberforce.* c. 1785. Wilberforce Museum, Hull.

After WILLIAM BEECHEY, *Rustic Charity: Here Poor Boy Without a Coat, Take This Halfpenny.* c. 1780. Mezzotint. British Museum, London.

A. F. BIARD, *The Slave Market.* Oil. Wilberforce Museum, Hull.

On Board a Slave Ship. Print.

Slave Hold. Watercolor. National Maritime Museum.

C. E. WAGSTUFF, *Woman Slave Being Branded.* Engraving after A. F. BIARD. Wilberforce Museum, Hull.

Model of a Slave Ship; shown to Parliament by Wilberforce. Wilberforce Museum, Hull.

GEORGE CRUIKSHANK, *Abolition of the Slave Trade.* 1834. Cartoon. British Museum, London.

J. HAYLLAR, *The Freed Slave.* Oil. Wilberforce Museum, Hull.

GUSTAVE DORÉ, *Over London by Rail.* 1872. Print.

Lancashire Cotton Mill. Print.

Power Loom Weaving. Print.

Mulespinning Cotton Mill. Print.

WRIGHT OF DERBY, *Portrait of Sir Richard Arkwright.* c. 1790. Oil, 7'10"x4'11". Captain Richard Arkwright Collection. Willersey, England.

Love Conquered Fear, illustration from *The Life and Adventures of Michael Armstrong.*

GEORGE ROBERTSON, *Nant-Y-Glo Iron Works.* National Museum of Wales, Cardiff.

PHILIPPE JACQUES DE LOUTHERBOURG, *Coalbrookdale by Night.* 1801. Oil. Science Museum, London.

Lymington Iron Works. Print.

FRANCIS NICHOLSON, *Explosion and Fire at Shiffnal.* 1820. Lithograph. British Museum, London.

In the Black Country around Wolverhampton. 1866. Print.

Industrial Landscape, Huddersfield, England.

LUKE FILDES, *Admission to a Casualty Ward.* 1874. Oil. Royal Holleway College, southwest of London.

GUSTAVE DORÉ, Montage of illustrations from *London, A Pilgrimage* by Blanchard Jerrold. 1872. Wood engravings: 1) Plate 158, *Dudley St. Seven Dials;* 2) Plate 124, *Wentworth Street;* 3) Plate 126, *Houndsditch;* 4) Plate 138, *Bluegate Fields;* 5) Plate 144, *The Bull's*

Eye; 6) Plate 180, *Refugee: Applying for Admittance;* 7) Plate 142, *Night Refuge.*

Newgate Prison Cell with Elizabeth Fry. c. 1830. Print.

Man in Shackles at Newgate. Color Print.

G. F. WATTS, *Portrait of Lord Shaftesbury.* c. 1850. Canvas, 23½ x 19½". National Portrait Gallery, London.

GUSTAVE DORÉ, Illustration from *London, A Pilgrimage.* 1872. Plate 158, *Dudley St. Seven Dials.*

Children's Ward at Great Ormond Street Hospital. Mid-19th century. Print.

Cedar Ward of Great Ormond Street Hospital, at Tadworth, Surrey, England.

A Military Flogging. 1844. Print.

Point of Honor. 19th century. Color print.

Shackles, etc., on board convict ship *Success.* 19th century. Photograph.

Caged Prisoners on Way to Australia. Print.

Bluebell Railway Line, Haywards Heath, England.

Travelling on the Manchester-Liverpool Railway. c. 1830. Color print.

Plate Layers Working on the Manchester-Liverpool Railway. 1831. Print.

Navvies at Crystal Palace. 1853. Photograph.

Launching of the Great Eastern, Transatlantic Steamship, detail showing Brunel and other engineers. Photograph. 1858.

ABRAHAM DARBY IV, iron bridge, near Coalbrookdale, Shropshire, western England. 1777-79. First cast-iron bridge of any size was constructed at Coalbrookdale ironworks, established by Abraham Darby I in 1708.

THOMAS TELFORD, *Menai Bridge.* 1820. Print.

ISEMBARD KINGDOM BRUNEL, Clifton Suspension Bridge, Bristol, England. 1836-64. Photograph.

Dinner in the Thames Tunnel with the Brunels, Father and Son. 1827. Lady Noble, Humshaugh.

GOODALL, *Flood in the Thames Tunnel.* 1830's. Lady Noble, Humshaugh.

Opening of Saltash Bridge, designed by Brunell. 1859. Color print.

Wharncliffe Viaduct for the Great Western Railway, designed by Brunel and completed in 1841. Print.

The Tunnel Islington for the Great Western Railway; Brunel, chief engineer; completed 1841. Print.

Kilsby Tunnel for the Great Western Railway; Brunel, chief engineer;

completed 1841. Print.

No. 1 Tunnel, Bristol, for the Great Western Railway; Brunel, chief engineer; completed 1841. Print.

Brunel standing against the chains of the Great Eastern Steamship. 1857. Photograph.

Montage of photos of Great Eastern Steamship, designed by Brunel. 1858.

JOHN FOWLER and BENJAMIN BAKER, Forth Rail Bridge, Firth of Forth, Scotland. 1883-90.

JOSEPH PAXTON, Crystal Palace. 1851. Photographs of interior and exterior, showing Great Exhibition of 1851.

JEAN FRANÇOIS MILLET, *The Gleaners,* 1857. Canvas, 33x44½". Louvre, Paris.

JEAN FRANÇOIS MILLET, *Man With the Hoe.* 1849. Provident Securities Company, San Francisco.

MATTHEW DIGBY WYATT, *Industrial Arts of the Nineteenth Century. . . . Illustrations of the Choicest Specimens . . . at the Great Exhibition.* 1851. Color illustration, Vol. 11, Plate 89.

GUSTAVE COURBET, *Bonjour, Monsieur Courbet.* 1854. Canvas. Musée Fabre, Montpellier.

GUSTAVE COURBET, *The Stonebreakers.*1849 (now destroyed). Canvas, 5'2⅝"x8'6". Formerly in Gemaldegalerie, Dresden (destroyed during World War II).

GUSTAVE COURBET, *Funeral at Ornans.* 1850. Canvas, 10'3½"x 21'9½". Louvre, Paris.

GEORGES SEURAT, *Bathers.* 1883-84. Canvas, 6'7"x9'10½". National Gallery, London.

PIERRE RENOIR, *Déjeuner des Canotiers (Luncheon of the Boating Party).* 1881. Canvas, 50½x68". Phillips Collection, Washington, D.C.

PIERRE RENOIR, *Moulin de la Galette.* 1876. Canvas, 4'3½"x5'8⅞". Musée du Jeu de Paume, Paris.

EDOUARD MANET, *The Bar at the Folies Bergère.* 1882. Canvas, 37¾ x 50". Courtauld Institute, London.

PIERRE RENOIR, *Dance at Bougival.* 1883. Canvas, 71x38½". Museum of Fine Arts, Boston.

VINCENT VAN GOGH, *Self-Portrait with Palette.* 1888. Canvas, 25½ x 20". Stedelijk Museum, Amsterdam.

VINCENT VAN GOGH, *Peasant Woman Pulling Up Grass.* 1883-85. Black chalk drawing, 19¼ x51". Folkwang Museum, Essen.

VINCENT VAN GOGH, *The Woodcutter*. 1883-85. Black chalk drawing, 17¼ x21½ ". Stedelijk Museum, Amsterdam.

VINCENT VAN GOGH, *Woman Digging*. 1883-85. Black chalk drawing, 21¾ x16". Stedelijk Musem, Amsterdam.

VINCENT VAN GOGH, *Peasant Reaping*. 1883-85. Black chalk drawing, 17¼ x22". Stedelijk Museum, Amsterdam.

VINCENT VAN GOGH, *Reaper*. 1883-85. Black chalk drawing, 16¼ x 20". Stedelijk Museum, Amsterdam.

VINCENT VAN GOGH, *Two Women and Wheelbarrow in Field*. 1883. Canvas, 10¾ x14". Stedelijk Museum, Amsterdam.

VINCENT VAN GOGH, *The Sower*. 1888. Canvas, 13x16½ ". Stedelijk Museum, Amsterdam.

Contemporaneous film and photographs of Tolstoy at Yasnaya Polyana, his home; Tolstoy's death at railway station of Astapovo, 1910.

Jodrell Bank radio telescopes, 1957 and 1964, at the Nuffield Radio-Astronomy laboratories of the University of Manchester, England.

YOUSUF KARSH, two photographs of Albert Einstein.

Montage of NASA and rocket films: rocket lift-off, hurricane over Florida from space, spacecraft over coast of California, India and Ceylon from space, the edge of the earth from space, astronaut working outside spacecraft, earth from space, surface of the moon filmed from spacecraft and the earth and moon from space.

Montage of industrial shots: oil spill at Fawley refinery, built 1951, southwestern England; piping at Fawley; Berkeley atomic power station, built 1961, western England; computer typewriter ball and computer tapes.

Montage of aviation and war films: test flight of the British-French airplane *Concorde;* air shot of stukas (dive bombers), World War II; bridge explosion; London fire raid, World War II; flaming streets in the Southwark district of London, World War II; fires around St. Paul's, London, World War II; atom bomb explosion; aerial view of Hiroshima, Japan.

DENYS LASDUN, University of East Anglia, Norwich, England. 1968. Shown are ten pyramidal dormitories, the library and the university plain.

MICHELANGELO, *Unfinished Slave*. 1532-34. Marble. Accademia, Florence.

MICHELANGELO, *Ceiling of the Sistine Chapel*, Vatican, Rome. 1508-12. Fresco.

Saltwood Castle, England. An estate which once belonged to the Archbishops of Canterbury; rendezvous of Becket's murderers, 1170.

Now owned by Kenneth Clark, Lord Clark of Saltwood. Shown: library with Henry Moore sculpture on table.

Important Names in Art and History

Abelard, Peter. 1079-1142. French philosopher, teacher and theologian, whose romance with Héloise, his pupil, is one of the famous stories of history.

Adam, Robert. 1728-92. Scottish architect. With his brothers, John, James, and William, he introduced a neoclassic style of decoration, adapted from ancient Roman stucco ornament. With James, Robert Adam built many public buildings and private mansions. Architect to George III, 1762-68.

Addison, Joseph. 1672-1719. English essayist, poet and statesman. Publisher, with Sir Richard Steele, of *The Spectator* in which some of his best social satire and literary criticism appeared.

Alberti, Leon Battista. 1404?-72. Florentine architect and writer on architecture and city planning. Author of *De re aedificatoria* in which he advocated the centrally-planned church which became the preferred form of the Renaissance church.

Alcuin of York. 735-804. English theologian and scholar, teacher and adviser of Charlemagne.

Aldus Manutius. 1450-1515. Italian printer and classical scholar. His Aldine Press produced the first Greek classical books at low cost, and designed italic type.

Alfred the Great. 849-99. King of the West Saxons, 871-99.

Antinoüs. The beautiful favorite of the Roman Emperor Hadrian (76-138). After his death, Antinoüs became the object of a cult and model for numerous busts and statues.

Arkwright, Sir Richard. 1732-92. English inventor of a spinning machine, patented 1769. He established huge cotton mills and helped start the factory system.

Asam, the Brothers. Bavarian architects and decorators. Cosmas Damian (1686-1739) and Egid Quirin (1692-1750). The elder, Cosmas, specialized in fresco painting, the younger in sculpture and stucco work. They created in their buildings an ingenious unity of architecture, sculpture and painting. Chief among their works are the Benedictine Church at Weltenburg (1717-21), the abbey Church at Rohr (1717-22) and St. Johann Nepomuk in Munich.

Augustus. 63 B.C.-14 A.D. First Roman emperor (27 B.C.-14A.D.); reformer, patron of arts and literature, heir and successor to Julius Caesar.

Austen, Jane. 1775-1817. English novelist; major works include *Pride and Prejudice, Sense and Sensibility* and *Mansfield Park.*

Bach, Johann Sebastian. 1685-1750. German Baroque composer. His many works include compositions for various instruments, keyboard and organ, sacred as well as secular cantatas.

Baciccia (Giovanni Battista Gaulli). 1639-1709. Genoese painter who worked in Rome; his major work is the ceiling of the Jesuit church, Il Gesù, in Rome.

Balzac, Honoré de. 1799-1850. French novelist. Explored the effects of social environment on the basic human personality. Attempted to portray a comprehensive picture of French society in *La Comédie Humaine* (published in 47 volumes).

Banks, Sir Joseph. 1743-1820. English naturalist. Accompanied Captain James Cook's expedition around the world 1768-71 in the *Endeavor*.

Barberini family. Roman noble family, art patrons; one member was Pope Urban VIII (see Urban VIII).

Barocci, Federico. 1526-1612. Central Italian painter, early Baroque in style.

Beethoven, Ludwig van. 1770-1827. German composer; the scope of his work, its technical richness and its depth of feeling make him unequaled among Romantic composers.

Bellini, Giovanni. c. 1430-1516. Venetian painter, one of three painters in the Bellini family. Giovanni is noted for his religious pictures with poetic landscape backgrounds.

Berckheyde, Gerrit. 1638-98. Haarlem painter of town views.

Bernini, Gianlorenzo. 1598-1680. Sculptor and architect, worked mainly in Rome, he is the chief source of the Baroque style in sculpture which is characterized by active figures and drapery and emotional religiosity.

Berry, Jean of France, Duke of. 1340-1416. An enlightened protector of the arts and artists, the Duke of Berry was also active in the political turmoil of his times. He made a vast collection of paintings, tapestries, jewelry and illuminated manuscripts. Of the latter the *Très Riches Heures* is an excellent record of his magnificent residences.

Black, Joseph. 1728-99. Scottish chemist and physician, best known for his theories of latent and specific heat.

Blake, William. 1757-1827. English poet, engraver and painter who illustrated his own books of poems, among them, *Songs of Innocence*. His many religious watercolors stem from a personal symbolism.

Blanche of Castille. 1185?-1252. Queen of Louis VIII of France, regent of her son Louis IX after his departure on Crusade.

Boccaccio, Giovanni. 1313-1375. Florentine writer and scholar. Author of *The Decameron*.

Boethius, Anicius Manlius Severinus. c. 475-525. Roman philosopher and statesman who wrote *De consolatione philosophiae (The Consolation of Philosophy)*.

Bohr, Niels. 1885-1962. Danish physicist who developed a concept of the structure of the atom which he reconciled with the quantum theory; worked on development of the atomic bomb.

Boilly, Louis Léopold. 1761-1845. French painter and engraver of portraits and historical and genre subjects.

Borghese family. Italian noble family which produced one pope, Paul V, and several cardinals, among them Cardinal Scipione Borghese who built the Villa Borghese in Rome and commissioned many of Bernini's important early works.

Borgia family. Spanish noble family; two members were Popes. Pope Alexander VI and his natural son, Cesare (1475-1507), general of the papal armies, used the papal position to aggrandize the family's land and power.

Borromini, Francesco. 1599-1667. Major Italian Baroque architect and innovator of Baroque forms. Official architect of Rome, 1644-55. A major work, Sant'Ivo della Sapienza, Rome, is a dynamic hexagonal structure.

Botticelli, Sandro. c. 1445-1510. Florentine painter, member of Neo-Platonist circle of intellectuals and poets who surrounded Lorenzo de' Medici. Known for his graceful Madonnas and mythological figures whose expressions are touched by melancholy. Among major works: *Spring, The Birth of Venus*.

Boucher, François. 1703-70. French Rococo painter, engraver and designer of tapestries. More than 1,000 pictures and studies testify to his activity and popularity.

Bougainville, Louis Antoine de. 1729-1811. French navigator. Accompanied by naturalists and astronomers, he made a voyage around the world, 1767-69. His description of Tahiti helped to popularize Rousseau's theories on the morality of man in the state of nature.

Boyle, Robert. 1627-91. British chemist who was first to distinguish between elements and compounds.

Bramante, Donato. 1444-1514. Architect of the Italian Renaissance who worked in Milan (1472-99) and in Rome (1499-1514). Employed by Popes Alexander VI and Julius II, for whom he drew up plans (carried out only in part) for the reconstruction of St. Peter's.

Bray, Jan de. 1626/7-97. Dutch painter of portraits and portrait groups.

Brown, Mather. 1750-1831. American painter known for his portraits of English royalty and other important figures.

Bruegel, Pieter. c. 1525/30-69. An important artist of the Netherlands known for his paintings of peasants. Often crowded with figures, his works satirized the drunkeness, gluttony and ribaldry of village life.

Brunel, Isambard Kingdom. 1806-59. English civil engineer and authority on railway traction and steam navigation. He was the engineer of the Great Western Railway, building its bridges and tunnels. He also designed three steamships, the last of which was the Great Eastern (1858).

Brunelleschi, Filippo. 1377-1446. Florentine architect and innovator of the pure, economical Florentine Renaissance style. Major works: Pazzi Chapel, Old Sacristy of San Lorenzo and the dome of the cathedral of Florence.

Bruni, Leonardo. 1370-1444. Humanist, chancellor to the Republic of Florence (1427-44). Author of *History of the Florentine People*.

Brutus, Lucius Junius. Roman consul, 509 B.C., one of the first in Roman history. According to legend, took leading part in expulsion of Tarquins (Roman despots) and sentenced his own two sons to death when they conspired to restore Tarquins. Subject of painting by David.

Burlington, Richard Boyle, Lord, Third Earl of Burlington and fourth Earl of Cork. 1694-1753. Statesman and patron of art and literature. Sponsored the Palladian revival in architecture in the 1720's; built Chiswick House with William Kent.

Burns, Robert. 1759-96. Scottish poet who depicted humble people in rural Scotland. Many of his songs and ballads are in Scottish dialect; among his best-loved are *Auld Lang Syne* and *Comin' thro' the Rye.*

Byrd, William. 1543-1623. English composer of both Anglican and Roman Catholic church music.

Byron, George Gordon, Lord. 1788-1824. Sixth Baron Byron. English romantic poet who became the ideal figure of his age. His stormy short life ended while fighting for Greek independence. Best known for long narrative poems such as *Childe Harold's Pilgrimage* and *Don Juan.*

Calas family. Family of Jean Calas (1698-1762), French Calvinist merchant wrongly convicted and executed for the murder of his son to prevent his becoming a Roman Catholic. The son died by suicide. Family harbored by Voltaire at Ferney.

Calvin, John. 1509-64. French theologian and reformer in Switzerland, leader in the Protestant Reformation. Calvin believed that the Bible is the sole source of God's law, man's duty being to interpret it and to preserve order in the world. Calvinism became the doctrine of Protestant "Reformed" churches, including the Presbyterian churches.

Cameron, Charles. c. 1740-1812. Scottish architect who lived in Russia after 1779. Decorated apartments at Tsarkoe Selo for Catherine the Great, built and remodeled other imperial residences in neoclassical style.

Caravaggio (Michelangelo Merisi). 1573-1610. Italian Baroque painter known for his realism and originality, his use of strong lights and darks (chiaroscuro) and his preference for contemporary, often humble, settings. Among major works: *Calling of St. Matthew, Madonna di Loreto* and *The Death of the Virgin.*

Castiglione, Baldassare. 1478-1529. Author of *The Book of the Courtier (Il Cortigiano),* a dialogue on Renaissance courtly manners and ideals. The setting of the book is the Court of Urbino where Castiglione lived from 1504-24.

Catlin, George. 1796-1872. American artist, traveller and author who devoted himself to the study of American Indians.

Chardin, Jean Baptiste Siméon. 1699-1779. French painter of simple still lifes and domestic interiors in muted tones with great feeling for arrangements and surfaces.

Charlemagne. 742-814. King of the Franks (768-814); as Charles I, Emperor of the Holy Roman Empire (800-814).

Charles Martel. 690?-741. Ruler of the Franks (714-41), grandfather of Charlemagne.

Charles II, King of England, Scotland and Ireland, of the Stuart house. 1630-85; reigned 1660-85. When the Civil War broke out, Charles, still a boy, fled to France (1646). When his father, Charles I, was beheaded in 1649 Cromwell became Protector. Charles returned in 1660 as Charles II.

Charles V, Holy Roman Emperor. 1500-1558. Charles I of Spain and Charles V of the Holy Roman Empire from 1519-50. Charles inherited an empire which included Spanish America, Spain, Naples, Sicily, the Low Countries and hereditary lands of Austria. His treasury was fed by gold from Spanish America, and he was the most wealthy and powerful monarch of Renaissance Europe.

Childeric I. 437?-481. Frankish king; father of Clovis. King of the Salian Franks (458?-481) with capital at Tournai.

Chrétien de Troyes. c. 1164. French poet, author of the first great literary treatments of the legend of King Arthur and his court.

Christina, Queen of Sweden. 1626-89. An irresponsible, eccentric ruler who devoted her time to the study of philosophy. In 1649 she brought Descartes to Sweden. She abdicated in 1654.

Cimabue, Giovanni. c. 1240-1302? Florentine painter and mosaicist, reputedly the teacher of Giotto. Frescoes, especially the *Crucifixions,* in the Church of St. Francis, Assisi, are attributed to him. His work is a transition from the formalized Byzantine style to the more naturalistic 14th-century manner.

Clarkson, Thomas. 1760-1846. English abolitionist. He wrote *Essay on Slavery* in 1786; worked with Wilberforce to abolish British slave trade.

Clement VII. c. 1475-1534. The Florentine Giulio de' Medici was Pope Clement VII from 1523-34. His papacy encompassed the growing strength of Lutheranism in the north (the famous 95 theses had been posted in 1517), the struggle with Henry VIII of England and the sack of Rome in 1527. He commissioned Michelangelo's Medici Chapel in Florence and the *Last Judgment* in the Sistine Chapel.

Clovis I. 465-511. King of the Franks (481-511). Founder of the Frankish monarchy and an important early convert to Christianity.

Coleridge, Samuel Taylor. 1772-1834. English poet and critic who saw nature as a mystic presence.

Colet, John. 1467?-1519. English humanist, friend of Erasmus and associate of Sir Thomas More; dean of St. Paul's Cathedral and planner of St. Paul's school.

Collins, William. 1721-59. English poet.

Colson, Jean François Gille. 1733-1803. French portrait painter, architect and sculptor.

Columbus, Christopher. 1446?-1506. Italian navigator in Spanish service, discoverer of America in 1492.

Cook, Captain James. 1728-79. English explorer and navigator, explored the south Pacific and Antarctic Oceans and was killed on the Hawaiian Islands.

Cortona, Pietro da. 1596-1669. Painter and architect of the Roman High Baroque; known for his spectacular ceilings, in particular the ceiling decoration in the Barberini Palace.

Courbet, Gustave. 1819-77. French painter of realistic portraits, landscapes and scenes in the lives of the common of people of Ornans, the village where he lived.

Coverdale, Miles. 1488-1569. English translator of the Bible, 1535. He was an advocate for church reform and an eloquent preacher.

Cozens, John Robert. 1752-97. English landscape watercolorist who worked mainly on the Continent, particularly in the Alps.

Cranach, Lucas, the Elder. 1472-1553. German painter, etcher and designer of woodcuts. He was court painter to three electors of Saxony and a friend and supporter of Martin Luther.

Cruikshank, George. 1792-1878. English caricaturist, illustrator and etcher. Among his works are *Life in London* (in collaboration with his brother) and illustrations for *Oliver Twist*.

Cuvilliés, François de. 1695-1768. Court dwarf appointed by Max Emmanuel; educated with the aristocracy, became architect to the Court in 1725 in Munich. His studies in Paris from 1720-24 exposed him to French Rococo. On his return to Bavaria he developed this style in the Munich Residenz and its various buildings.

Dante Alighieri. 1265-1321. Italian poet and author of *The Divine Comedy*, an epic poem in which the narrator is led by Vergil through Hell and Purgatory, and by Beatrice, his ideal, through Paradise.

Daumier, Honoré. 1808-79. French caricaturist, painter and sculptor, best known for his lithographs which mercilessly ridiculed bourgeois society of his time.

David, Jacques Louis. 1748-1825. French painter of allegory, history, mythology and portraits; court painter to Napoleon for whom he painted large compositions of contemporary historical events.

Debussy, Claude Achille. 1862-1918. French composer, exponent of musical impressionism.

Deffand, Marquise du. 1697-1780. French noblewoman, leader in social life, remembered chiefly for her friendship and correspondence with noted men, including Voltaire.

Demachy, Pierre Antoine. 1723-1807. French painter and engraver of historical and architectural subjects.

De Quincey, Thomas. 1785-1859. English essayist who wrote *Confessions of an English Opium Eater*.

Descartes, René. 1596-1650. French philosopher, mathematician and scientist. In *Discourse on Method* he doubted everything but doubt itself; the act of doubting led to: "I think, therefore I am." On this premise he built a new philosophy and proved by logic the existence of God.

Devis, Arthur. 1711-87. English painter of portraits and conversation pieces (group portraits of an informal character).

Dickens, Charles. 1812-70. English novelist and social critic. His popular novels are outstanding for their descriptions of eccentric characters and for their depictions of social evils, in particular, imprisonment for debt, legal delay, ill treatment of orphans and bad schools. His novels include *David Copperfield* (1850), *Bleak House* (1853) and *Great Expectations* (1861).

Diderot, Denis. 1713-84. French philosopher, writer and leading figure of the Enlightment. Compiled, with d'Alembert and others, the *Encyclopédie*. Also wrote plays, art criticism, and novels.

Donatello. 1386-1466. Greatest Florentine sculptor before Michelangelo.

Doré, Paul Gustave. 1832-83. French painter and illustrator. He had a keen eye for social distress. Among his better-known book illustrations are Cervantes's *Don Quixote* and Balzac's *Contes Drôlatiques*.

Dowland, John. 1563-1626. English lutenist and composer of songs.

Dürer, Albrecht. 1471-1528. German painter and engraver. His diverse interests in the fields of the humanities and mathematics and his scholarly friendship were common among artists in Italy but unusual in Germany. Through him Italian Renaissance forms and ideas were introduced to northern Europe. His prints, woodcuts and engravings were widely distributed throughout Europe.

Einstein, Albert. 1879-1955. American theoretical physicist, formulated theory of relativity. He saw gravitation as a determiner of curvature of the space-time continuum.

Engels, Friedrich. 1820-95. German socialist and organizer of revolutionary groups, writer, co-founder with Karl Marx of Marxist communism. Engels wrote *The Condition of the Working Class in England* in 1844 and collaborated with Marx on *The Communist Manifesto* (1848).

Erasmus, Desiderius. 1466?-1536. Dutch humanist, theologian, scholar and writer. He was an advocate of church reforms. His major work is the satirical *Praise of Folly* (1509).

Euclid. Lived c. 300 B.C. Greek geometrician and educator at Alexandria.

Evelyn, John. 1620-1706. English diarist.

Farnese family. Italian noble family, art patrons. In 1534 Alessandro Farnese became Pope Paul III, and created the duchy of Parma out of papal lands in northern Italy which his family ruled until 1731.

Flamsteed, John. 1646-1719. English astronomer, compiler of constellations and stars.

Fontenelle, Bernard le Borier de. 1657-1757. French man of letters, author of poems, operas, tragedies and essays on science; secretary of the Royal Academy of Science for over forty years.

Fragonard, Jean Honoré. 1732-1806. French painter and engraver known for his sensual style, subject matter and graceful, floating figures.

Freud, Sigmund. 1856-1939. Austrian psychiatrist, founder of psychoanalysis. Author of *Interpretation of Dreams* and *The Ego and the Id*.

Friedrich, Caspar David. 1774-1840. German landscape painter, known for paintings of forests with different effects of light and season.

Fry, Elizabeth. 1780-1845. English prison reformer who worked to improve the conditions of the women prisoners at Newgate, London.

Gainsborough, Thomas. 1727-88. English portraitist and landscape painter whose pastoral scenes are a synthesis of Dutch subjects—cows, streams and peasants—with French Rococo grace in a highly personal style.

Galileo. 1564-1642. Italian astronomer, mathematician and physicist, whose formulations foreshadowed Newton's laws of motion and gravitation. He is believed to have constructed the first complete telescope (1609) but was forced by the Inquisition to recant his belief that the earth moved around the sun.

Gattamelata (Erasmo da Narni). Early 15th-century commander of the Venetian armies.

Geofforn, Marie Thérèse. 1699-1777. French patroness of literature; maintained a famous salon frequented by literary and artistic people.

Géricault, Théodore. 1791-1824. French painter. His bold composition, unorthodox coloring and attempt to achieve authenticity had great effect on the artists of the Romantic movement. Probably his best known work is *Raft of the Medusa*, 1818-19.

Ghiberti, Lorenzo. 1378-1455. Florentine sculptor who made two of the three bronze doors of the Baptistry in Florence (the first was made by Andrea Pisano, 1330). Ghiberti's first door shows scenes from the New Testament; the second, with Old Testament scenes, became known as the "Gates of Paradise."

Gibbon, Edward. 1737-94. English historian, author of monumental *Decline and Fall of the Roman Empire*.

Giorgione (Giorgio da Castelfranco). 1475/6-1510. Venetian painter who was a founder of the High Renaissance style. His subjects were frequently evocative and mysterious.

Giotto. 1266?-1337. Florentine painter, sculptor and architect; with Cimabue, regarded in the 15th century as the founder of modern painting. He turned from the conventional Byzantine style to the study of nature, achieving lifelike, expressive faces and three-dimensional form. His earliest extant works are in the Church of St. Francis, Assisi; his most famous are the Biblical frescoes in the Scrovegni (Arena) Chapel, Padua.

Girodet-Trioson, Anne Louis. 1767-1824. French painter, a favorite artist of Napoleon.

Gislebertus. French artist who carried out the sculptural decoration of the cathedral of Autun. His tympanum of the Last Judgment is one of the finest expressions of the despair and agony of damned souls in Romanesque art.

Giulio Romano. c. 1492-1546. Italian painter, architect and decorator who was the favorite pupil of Raphael.

Goethe, Johann Wolfgang von. 1749-1832. German poet, novelist, dramatist and scientist. His moral drama, *Faust*, plots the damnation and eventual salvation of a hero who is symbolically everyman.

Gogh, Vincent van. 1853-90. Dutch painter, worked in France. Early works show peasants and factory workers among whom he lived; at Arles in southern France he painted brilliantly colored landscapes and portraits.

Gonzaga, Francesco, Marquis of Mantua. 1466-1519. A noted Italian patriot, he attempted to curtail French intervention at the Battle of Taro (1495). His wife, Isabella, had a small but choice collection of art.

Goya, Francisco José de. 1746-1828. Great Spanish artist. His paintings, etchings and lithographs are among the great works of art of the period. He was court painter to the Spanish king, but he sympathized with the ideals of the French Revolution. His later works reflect the disillusionment of those Spaniards who had looked to France to bring them liberty.

Gozzoli, Benozzo. 1420-97. A Florentine painter whose greatest work is *The Procession of the Magi*, frescoes in the Palazzo Medici-Riccardi, Florence.

Gray, Thomas. 1761-71. English poet, forerunner of the Romantic movement in poetry; his famous "Elegy Written in a Country Churchyard" is a meditative poem with a rural setting.

Guercino (Giovanni Barbieri). 1591-1666. Italian painter who worked in Rome and Bologna.

Gutenberg, Johann. c. 1397-1468. German printer generally credited with the invention of printing from movable type. He printed the Mazarin, or Gutenberg, Bible around 1456 in Mainz, probably the first large book printed with movable type.

Hadrian. 76-138. Roman Emperor (117-138). Built a huge mausoleum in Rome, now the Castel Sant' Angelo.

Haldane, J. B. S. 1892-1964. British biochemist, geneticist and writer of science books for the layman.

Halley, Edmund. 1656-1742. English astronomer, astronomer royal from 1720. First to predict the return of a comet (Halley's comet).

Hals, Frans. 1580/85-1666. Portrait painter of Harlem, Holland. His group portraits give a sense of corporate or civic Dutch life.

Handel, George Frederic. 1685-1759. German-English composer. After travelling through Germany and Italy Handel settled in England in 1712. Handel's musical style is late Baroque with a distinctly English flavor. His great oratorio, *The Messiah*, was presented in Dublin in 1742.

Harun al-Rashid. 764?-809. Caliph of Baghdad (786-809) and legendary hero of *The Arabian Nights*.

Hawksmoor, Nicholas. 1661-1736. British architect, pupil of Wren, who helped Vanbrugh to complete Wren's designs at Greenwich. Hawksmoor designed Easton Neston, Northamptonshire, and assisted Vanbrugh in the building of Blenheim Palace.

Haydn, Franz Joseph. 1732-1809. Austrian composer. Most of his music was composed in the 29 years he was musical director for the Princes Esterhazy. He was a close friend of Mozart who was influenced by Haydn's early string quartets. He wrote over 100 symphonies; his last great works were two oratorios, *The Creation* and *The Seasons*.

Henry IV (Henry of Navarre). 1553-1610. First Bourbon king of France (1589-1610).

Hodges, Charles Howard. 1764-1837. British painter who went with Cook around the world.

Hogarth, William. 1697-1764. English painter and engraver. His series of moral subjects, which he engraved after his own paintings, *The Harlot's Progress, The Rake's Progress*, and *Marriage à la Mode*, are full of details which give a vivid picture of the more sordid side of 18th-century London life.

Holbein, Hans, the Younger. 1497?-1543. German painter, outstanding portrait painter of the German Renaissance. A good friend of Erasmus, he illustrated the latter's *Praise of Folly* and painted many portraits of him, of Sir Thomas More and eminent people. Painter to Henry VIII.

Hooch, Pieter de. 1629-after 1684. Dutch genre painter who came nearest to Vermeer in his feeling for light. He painted interiors with two or three figures engaged in a household task or an entertainment.

Horatii. In Roman legend, three brothers who represented Rome in a battle with Alba; they took an oath on their swords, in the presence of their father, to win or to die for liberty. Subject of painting by David.

Houdon, Jean Antoine. 1741-1828. French sculptor of classical figures and portrait statues, many of famous people of the period.

Howard, John. 1726-90. English prison reformer who worked to improve sanitary conditions and secure humane treatment.

Huber, Jean. 1721-1786. Swiss painter and engraver known for his works related to the life of Voltaire.

Hume, David. 1711-76. Scottish philosopher and historian, known for his philosophical skepticism; greatly influenced subsequent metaphysical thought. Wrote *A Treatise on Human Nature,* 1739, and other philosophical and historical works.

Huygens, Christian. 1629-95. Dutch mathematician and physicist. He developed the pendulum clock, improved telescopic lenses and discovered the rings of Saturn.

Huysum, Jan van. 1682-1749. Dutch flower painter, son of the flower painter Justus van Huysum. His paintings are highly detailed and rich in color.

Ingres, Jean August Dominique. 1780-1867. Leader of the French classical school of painting, known for his portraits and historical subjects.

Jefferson, Thomas. 1743-1826. Third president of the United States (1801-09) and important American architect; wished to be remembered as the author of the Declaration of Independence, of the Virginia statute for religious freedom and as the father of the University of Virginia.

Johnson, Dr. Samuel. 1709-84. English lexicographer, critic, poet and conversationalist. He wrote moral essays on the foibles of human nature, the *Lives of the Poets,* and what is considered the first great English dictionary. His life and many witty remarks are chronicled by the Scotch writer, James Boswell.

Julius II. 1443-1513. Giuliano della Rovere was created cardinal by his uncle, Sixtus IV, and elected pope in 1503. He was a warrior who completed the restoration of the Papal States to the Church and took an active part in the Italian wars. He commissioned the building of the new St. Peter's.

Justinian I. 483-565. Byzantine emperor (527-65) whose reign was a rebirth of imperial greatness emphasizing the supremacy of the emperor over the Church. His chief accomplishment was the codification of Roman law.

Kneller, Sir Godfrey. 1646-1723. German-born portrait painter who worked in England, painting royal personages and celebrities.

La Fontaine, Jean de. 1621-95. French writer of fables, published as *Fables Choisies, Mises en Vers* (1668-94). Consists of twelve books of some 230 fables drawn largely from Aesop. Each is a short tale of beasts behaving like men; many are sophisticated satires on French society of the time.

Lanfranc. 1005?-89. Italian Roman Catholic prelate and scholar in England; Archbishop of Canterbury, 1070-89.

Lange, Joseph. 1751-1831. Painter and actor born in Würzburg. He painted portraits of a number of famous actors. His portrait of his brother-in-law, Wolfgang Amadeus Mozart, is widely known.

Largillière, Nicolas de. 1656-1746. French painter, known particularly for portraits.

Latour, Maurice Quentin de. 1704-88. French painter, best known for lively pastel portraits.

Latrobe, Benjamin Henry. 1764-1820. English-born architect and engineer who worked in America. Among his works were the Bank of Pennsylvania building in Philadelphia, the first city water supply in America (Philadelphia, 1799), south wing of the Capitol in Washington and alterations on other Washington buildings including the White House.

Laurana, Francesco. c. 1430-1502? Fortress builder, sculptor and architect.

Law, John. 1671-1729. Scottish financier and speculator, originator of the so-called Mississippi Scheme that collapsed (1720) when too much paper currency was issued.

Leeuwenhoek, Anthony van. 1632-1723. Dutch scientist. He made a simple microscope and was the first to see protozoa and bacteria.

Leonardo da Vinci. 1452-1519. Italian painter, sculptor, architect, musician, engineer and scientist who is considered the supreme example of Renaissance genius. The richness and originality of his intellect is best revealed to us in his drawings and notebooks; his most famous painting is the *Mona Lisa* in the Louvre.

Limbourg, Pol, Herman and Jehanequin de. Flemish painters born after 1385 in Nijmegen, died after 1416. From 1411 court painters of the Duke of Berry for whom they made the most splendid of all his manuscripts, the *Très Riches Heures du Duc de Berry*, one of the great achievements of the International Gothic Style, showing a new realism in detail of landscape, animals and costume .

Livy. Roman historian. 59 B.C.-17 A.D.

Locke, John. 1632-1704. English philosopher. His great work, written over seventeen years, was *An Essay Concerning Human Understanding* (1690), an attempt to resolve which questions were the proper concern of the human intellect.

Lothair I. 795-855. Frankish emperor of the Carolingian dynasty and half-brother of Charles the Bald.

Louis XIV. 1638-1715. King of France (1643-1715). Called the Sun King. He brought the Bourbon monarchy to its peak. The century of Louis XIV is the great classical age of French culture. Louis was a generous and discerning patron. The pomp and etiquette surrounding his life at Versailles symbolized the almost divine dignity to which he had raised the office of the king.

Loutherbourg, Philippe Jacques de. 1740-1812. Landscape and theatrical scene painter who was born in Strasbourg and worked in England.

Luther, Martin. 1483-1546. German leader of Protestant Reformation who broke away from the Catholic church because of doctrinal differences and corruption of higher circles of the church. Lutheranism taught that a sinner's hope lay entirely in his faith in the grace of God and redemption by Christ.

Machiavelli, Niccolò. 1469-1527. Florentine statesman and author of *The Prince,* a treatise on government and diplomacy in which he analyzed realistically and amorally the methods by which political power is obtained and kept.

Macpherson, James. 1736-96. Scottish schoolmaster and self-proclaimed translator of *The Romantic Poems of Ossian* which he actually wrote, but claimed were of the third century. Published *Fingal, an Ancient Epic* (1761).

Malatesta, Sigismondo. d. 1467. Called the "Wolf of Rimini," he was the tyrant of Rimini, a town in northeast Italy. He combined unscrupulousness, impiety, military skill and high culture.

Mallet, Jean Baptiste. 1759-1835. French painter and engraver; known especially for his watercolor and gouache works.

Malory, Sir Thomas. c. 1400-71. English author of *Morte d'Arthur,* last medieval English treatment of the legend of King Arthur.

Malthus, Thomas Robert. 1766-1834. English economist and pioneer demographist. In *An Essay on the Principles of Population* (1798), he contended that poverty was unavoidable since population increases by geometrical ratio and means of subsistence by arithmetical ratio. When population growth mushroomed, it would be checked by famine, disease and war. In his revised edition (1803) he admitted also the preventive check of "moral restraint."

Manetti, Giannozzo. 1393-1459. Florentine humanist and statesman who wrote *On the Dignity and Excellence of Man.*

Mantegna, Andrea. c. 1431-1506. North Italian artist who was court painter at Mantua. Among major works: frescoes in Ovetari Chapel in the Eremitani Church, Padua (destroyed); frescoes in Camera degli Sposi, Mantua.

Marat, Jean Paul. 1743-93. French revolutionist, physician and scientist. Founded, in 1789, the journal *L'Ami du peuple* (The Friend of the People) in which he attacked political leaders; his articles were instrumental in overthrowing the monarchy in 1792. He was murdered in his bath by Charlotte Corday, a political enemy.

Marcus Aurelius. 121-180. Roman Emperor, 161-180, and Stoic philosopher.

Marlborough, first Duke of (John Churchill). 1650-1722. British military commander. After the victory of Blenheim in Bavaria, during the War of the Spanish Succession, he was rewarded with a palace in Oxfordshire (See Blenheim Palace).

Marlowe, Christopher. 1564-93. English dramatist; first to discover the strength and variety of blank verse in *Tamburlaine the Great,* a play about the medieval Mongol conqueror of the East. Author also of the *Tragedy of Dr. Faustus.*

Marx, Karl. 1818-83. German social philosopher, economist and chief theorist of modern socialism. His major work *Das Kapital,* 1867-97, is the foundation of communist theory and of the Marxist view of history.

Masaccio (Tommaso di Ser Giovanni di Mone). 1401-28? First of a succession of great painters in 15th-century Florence, he painted figures of recognizable bulk whose positions in space were determined by light and by the laws of linear perspective.

Matisse, Henri. 1869-1954. French painter who began as one of the originators of Fauvism, a movement in painting marked by bold distortion and vivid color directed to the emotions. A leading 20th-century painter and designer of the chapel of St. Marie du Rosaire at Vence, near Nice, France, in 1948-51.

Max Emmanuel, Elector of Bavaria (Maximilian II). 1662-1726. During the last 20 years of his life in Munich, Max Emmanuel was able to indulge his passion for building. He preferred Italian and French art and succeeded in imposing the Regency style on his country during these 20 years. It was he who recognized the genius Cuvilliés and had him trained to become an architect.

Medici. Italian merchant and banking family which directed the destinies of Florence from the 15th to 18th centuries; produced three popes (Leo X, Clement VII, and Leo XI), two queens of France (Catherine de' Medici and Marie de' Medici) and several cardinals of the Roman church. During the Renaissance they were great patrons of the arts. Cosimo de' Medici. 1389-1464. Wealthy merchant, party leader and patron of arts, he built the library of San Marco. He was the grandfather of Lorenzo the Magnificent. Lorenzo de' Medici, (the Magnificent). 1449-92. Heir to the wealthiest and most influential banking house in Florence; ruler of Florence, 1469-92; poet, politician of genius and patron of the arts.

Melozzo da Forlí. 1438-94. Painter of north central Italy noted for frescoes with full-bodied figures in splendid architectural settings.

Metzu, Gabriel. 1629-67. Dutch painter of domestic interiors and genre scenes.

Michelangelo. Michelangelo Buonarroti. 1475-1564. Italian sculptor, painter, architect and poet of the High Renaissance. His great works include: in sculpture, *David, Moses* and the *Slaves* for the tomb of Julius II, the Medici Chapel in Florence; in painting, the Sistine Ceiling; and in architecture, the Campidoglio and his designs for St. Peter's.

Millet, Jean François. 1814-75. French painter. In 1849 he settled in Barbizon where he painted peasants and simple rural scenes.

Milton, John. 1608-74. English poet. He wrote the epic poem, *Paradise Lost* (1667), which recounts Satan's rebellion against God and the fall of Adam and Eve.

Molière, pseudonym of Jean Baptiste Poquelin. 1622-73. French actor and playwright. Formed own company, known after receiving patronage of Louis XIV as the King's Comedians. Wrote many comedies, including *Le Misanthrope* (1666) and *Tartuffe* (1669).

Mondrian, Piet. 1872-1944. Dutch abstract painter of severe geometric shapes and lines.

Monet, Claude. 1840-1926. Leader of the French Impressionists who painted outdoors and studied the effect of light on color. Monet's style is characterized by broken brushwork and light, fresh color.

Montaigne, Michel Eyquem, Seigneur de. 1533-92. French author, whose

Essais are considered among the finest essays ever written and had an incalculable influence on European literature.

Montefeltro, Federigo da. 1444-82. First Duke of Urbino, greatest general of his day, builder and benefactor of his people and head of one of the model courts of Renaissance Italy. The court of his son, Guidobaldo, the second duke, was immortalized by Baldassare Castiglione in *The Book of the Courtier*.

Montesquieu, Charles Louis de Secondat, Baron de la Brède et de Montesquieu. 1689-1755. French political philosopher. He wrote *The Persian Letters*, a satire on the French court, and the monumental *Spirit of Laws* from which our idea of the balance of power is derived.

Monteverdi, Claudio. 1567-1643. Italian composer, first great name in operatic history. He defended expressive use of dissonances and wrote operas, e.g. *Orfeo*, and madrigals and religious music.

More, Sir Thomas. 1478-1535. Author of *Utopia*, More was an English statesman and humanist, saint and martyr in the Roman Catholic Church. *Utopia* is a picture of an ideal state based entirely on reason.

Moreau, Jean Michel. Called Moreau Le Jeune. 1741-1814. French engraver and illustrator. Engraved, with other artists, a series on French fashion known as the Monument of Costume (c. 1780) and illustrated many literary works.

Mozart, Wolfgang Amadeus. 1756-91. Austrian composer born in Salzburg. Mozart was a child prodigy who played the harpsichord, violin and organ at court and in aristocratic circles throughout Europe. He became imperial chamber musician and court composer in 1787. Although he died at the age of 34 he composed over 600 works including operas, oratorios, symphonies and chamber music.

Napoleon Bonaparte. 1769-1821. Corsican-born French general who won many victories in the Revolutionary Wars before overthrowing the French Directory on the 18th Brumaire (November 9), 1799. Promulgated new Constitution for France and became First Consul (December, 1799); in 1804 France declared a hereditary empire; Bonaparte reigned as Emperor Napoleon from December 1804 to 1814. Under his rule the boundaries of France were extended, the Catholic Church was restored to its position before the Revolution, the laws of France were codified (*Code Napoléon*, 1804-10), the government was completely reorganized and the educational system restructured. Conquered most of continental Europe but was finally defeated by the Sixth Coalition of European powers. Abdicated and sent to Elba (1814), Louis XVIII placed on the throne by Coalition powers; Napoleon escaped, returning to Paris in March, 1815, to rule for the Hundred Days; defeated again at Waterloo and exiled to the island of St. Helena.

Nattier, Jean Marc. 1685-1766. French painter of portraits and historical subjects.

Neumann, Johann Balthasar. 1687-1753. German architect. He designed several palaces and churches in Würzburg. In 1742 he began the planning of the most famous Rococo church of Germany, called Vierzehnheiligen, celebrated for the sumptuous architectural decoration of the interior within a series of oval spaces. Neumann was the architect to the Schönborn family; his first major commission was the Würzburg Residenz.

Newton, Sir Isaac. 1642-1727. English natural philosopher and mathematician, credited with invention of differential and integral calculus; conceived the theory of universal gravitation and formulated the laws of motion in his *Principia* (1687); published his optical experiments in *Optics* (1704). One of the great scientific minds of the modern world.

Nietzsche, Friedrich Wilhelm. 1844-1900. German philosopher. In his work *Thus Spake Zarathustra* (1883, 1891) he condemns traditional Christian morality as the code of the slavish masses and preaches the superiority of the natural aristocrat whose actions arise from the will to power and are beyond good and evil.

Niobe. In Greek mythology, queen of Thebes whose children were killed to punish her. A Greek figure of the dying son of Niobe was an inspiration for Michelangelo's statue of the *Dying Slave*.

Ollivier, Michel Barthélemy. 1712-84. French painter and engraver. Known for his delicate style; painted portraits, genre subjects and landscapes.

Ossian. Legendary Irish warrior and alleged author of Gaelic poems, including Fingal (1761), which James Macpherson claimed to have found.

Ovid. 43 B.C.–17? A.D. Roman poet who wrote *The Art of Love* and *The Metamorphoses,* mythological tales and legends in verse.

Palladio, Andrea. Italian architect, 1518-80. Adapted principles of Roman architecture with dignity and grace in such buildings as Villa Rotonda, Vicenza (begun 1550). Had great influence on later architects especially in 18th-century England. (see Lord Burlington).

Pannini, Giovanni Paolo. c. 1692-1765/8. Roman painter of landscape, city scenes and ruins.

Pater, Walter Horatio. 1839-94. English essayist and critic, who taught at Brasenose College, Oxford. He was the leader of a movement stressing the moral importance of artistic perfection. Among his works are *Studies in the History of the Renaissance* (1873) and *Marius the Epicurean* (1885).

Paul III (Alessandro Farnese). 1468-1549. As Pope (1534-49) he sanctioned the Jesuit order and instituted the Council of Trent. Patron of Michelangelo and Raphael. (see Jesuit order, Council of Trent, and Farnese family.)

Paxton, Sir Joseph. 1808-65. British architect; builder of greenhouses and gardens. He designed the Crystal Palace, which housed the International Exhibition of 1851, entirely of glass and iron.

Pepys, Samuel. 1633-1703. English diarist; secretary to the admiralty 1672-79, 1684-89); president of the Royal Society, 1684. His diary, first published in 1825, gives an intimate picture of domestic, social and political life from 1660 to 1669.

Perroneau, Jean Baptiste. 1715-83. French painter and pastelist.

Petrarch. 1304-74. Italian poet, lover of nature and perfecter of the sonnet form, who did much to revive the spirit of antiquity through his works.

His well-known *Rime* are sonnets to his ideal, Laura.

Philippoteaux, Henri Félix Emmanuel. 1815-84. French painter, engraver and illustrator.

Piero della Francesca. 1410-1492. Central Italian painter and mathematician. Admired for his spacious, sculptural compositions. Major work: fresco cycle, *Story of the True Cross,* in the choir of St. Francesco at

Pinturicchio. c. 1454-1513. Umbrian mural painter who decorated Piccolomini Library in Siena and the Borgia apartments of Alexander VI in the Vatican.

Pisano, Giovanni. 1245/50-after 1314. Sculptor and architect. Pulpit in San Andrea, Pistoia, was completed in 1301. Last and greatest of the pulpits is in Pisa Cathedral. He was influenced by the French, working toward a new and personal synthesis of Gothic and classical elements.

Pisano, Nicola. c. 1220-84? With his son, Giovanni, among the leading Italian medieval sculptors. Many works are attributed to them either individually or in collaboration, including four great pulpits for which they are best known. The first of these is by Nicola, dated 1260, in the Baptistry at Pisa.

Platina (Bartolommeo de' Sacchi, called Platina) 1421-81. Italian humanist and historian who was appointed Vatican librarian by Sixtus IV. Among his works is the *History of the Lives of the Popes,* 1479.

Plato. 427?-347? B.C. Greek philosopher, student of Socrates. Plato was the founder of philosophic idealism; he wrote dialogues on law, justice and the *Republic,* which describes the perfect state ruled by a philosopher.

Plutarch. c. 46-c. 120. Greek biographer, author of *Lives of the Noble Grecians and Romans*, a collection of 46 short biographies of the leading political figures of ancient Greece and Rome.

Poliziano, Angelo. 1454-1494. Italian poet and member of the Florentine Neo-Platonic circle. He wrote *Stanze per la Giostra del Magnifico Giuliano de' Medici* (1475-78), which was the literary inspiration for Botticelli's painting *Birth of Venus.*

Pollock, Jackson. 1912-1956. American action painter. He created his works by dropping and spattering paint on canvas on the floor.

Pope, Alexander. 1688-1744. English poet known for his satires on eighteenth-century manners and morals.

Porta, Giacomo della. c. 1540-1602. Italian architect, completed dome of St. Peter's.

Potter, Paulus. 1625-54. Dutch animal painter. His most famous painting is the life-sized, highly detailed *Bull.*

Pozzo, Andrea. 1642-1709. Italian Baroque painter. His ceiling for Sant' Ignazio in Rome became the prototype for German baroque church and palace decoration.

Proust, Marcel. 1871-1922. French author of *Remembrance of Things Past* (1922-32), in which the author searches for his identity by remembering moments from the past.

Purcell, Henry. 1659-95. English composer; organist at Westminster Abbey, 1679-95.

Pushkin, Alexander Sergeevich. 1799-1837. Russian poet. Held office in

Russian government, but was dismissed because of his liberal views. Admired Byron's verse. Author of *Eugene Onegin, Boris Gudunov* and *The Queen of Spades.* Killed in a duel.

Pythagoras. c. 582-c. 500 B.C. Greek philosopher, mathematician, and religious reformer.

Ramsay, Allan. 1713-84. Scottish portraitist; court painter to George III of England.

Raphael. Raffaello Santi. 1483-1520. Italian painter, one of the great artists of the High Renaissance, who worked in Florence and, after 1508, in Rome in the service of Pope Julius II. Later, as a protégé of Pope Leo X, he was appointed chief architect of St. Peter's.

Récamier, Juliette. 1777-1849. French society beauty; her fashionable salon was a gathering place for influential political and literary figures. Painted by David.

Rembrandt van Rijn. 1606-69. Dutch painter and graphic artist. He painted religious and contemporary subjects, nudes, landscapes and portraits. Rembrandt is admired for the psychological insight of his portraits and the pathos of his religious scenes.

Reni, Guido. 1575-1642. Italian Baroque painter who worked in Rome and Bologna.

Renoir, Pierre Auguste. 1841-1919. French Impressionist painter. He painted landscapes in high key, buxom pink nudes and mothers and graceful children in outdoor settings.

Ricardo, David. 1772-1823. British economist. He held that wages cannot rise above the lowest level necessary for subsistence, and that the value of goods is measured by the amount of labor involved in their production. His chief work was *Principles of Political Economy and Taxation,* 1817.

Richelieu, Armand-Jean du Plessis, Duke of. 1585-1642. French statesman and cardinal. He became chief minister in 1624. He founded French Absolutism, broke the power of the Protestant Huguenots, and kept the recalcitrant nobles under control.

Riemenschneider, Tilman. c. 1460-1531. German sculptor, transitional to Renaissance, who worked in stone and wood. His slender figures are delicately carved, with expressive faces and Gothic grace.

Robbia, Luca della. 1400-82. Florentine sculptor, known for his pioneering work in glazed terra-cotta.

Robert, Hubert. 1733-1808. French painter, best known for architectural subjects, often ruins of buildings in the process of demolition.

Robespierre, Maximilien. 1758-94. One of the leading figures of the French Revolution. In 1793 he inaugurated, with the Committee of Public Safety then governing France, the Reign of Terror to combat the dangers of internal disunity. Attempted to establish a new civic religion. After much criticism of his rule, Robespierre was arrested on July 27, 1794, and guillotined the next day.

Rodin, Auguste. 1840-1917. The most celebrated sculptor of the late 19th century. He created a new form of sculpture using the fragment as a finished work, sometimes a head and trunk and a pair of hands that expressed emotion and movement. Among his best known works are *The Thinker,* the *Burghers of Calais, The Kiss* and *Balzac.* He made his figures, usually small size, in wax or plaster; later they were cut in marble or cast in bronze on a larger scale. Often, several casts of each work exist.

Roslin, Alexandre. 1718-95. Swedish portrait painter, worked in Paris.

Rousseau, Jean Jacques. 1712-1778. French philosopher, novelist and writer. He was a great innovator; his concepts of democracy profoundly influenced the development of French, Continental and American law and government. He was a champion of nature which for him meant many things including man before the institution of society, man stripped of social distinction and the out-of-doors, particularly mountains. His best known political works are the *Discourse on the Origin of Inequality of Men,* 1754, and *The Social Contract,* 1762.

Rubens, Peter Paul. 1577-1640. Flemish painter, noted for his Baroque religious and mythological painting. Rubens painted portraits and decorated palaces and halls and altarpieces. He worked in France, England and Spain, as well as in Flanders. Among major works are the Marie de' Medici series for the Luxembourg Palace in Paris (now in the Louvre), and the great altarpieces of *The Elevation of the Cross* and *The Descent from the Cross* in the Antwerp Cathedral.

Ruisdael, Jacob van. 1628/9-82. Dutch landscape painter. His realistic scenes of woods and pastures with vast, cloudswept skies are full of mood; they inspired the Romantic painters of the late 18th and early 19th centuries.

Ruskin, John. 1819-1900. British painter, critic and art historian who wrote *Modern Painters* (1843-60) in defense of Turner; in it he stated his thesis that art is based on rational and individual integrity and morality. He accumulated observations of plants, rocks, clouds and mountains in order to prove nature worked according to laws.

Rutherford, Ernest. 1871-1937. British physicist. His research in radioactivity contributed to the knowledge of the structure of the atom.

Sade, Donatien Alphonse François, Marquis de. 1740-1814. French writer best known for *Philosophy of the Boudoir.* Sade believed that since both sexual deviation and criminal acts exist in nature they must be natural.

Saenredam, Pieter. 1597-1665. Dutch painter of church interiors.

St. Anselm. 1033-1109. Archbishop of Canterbury; scholastic, theologian and philosopher.

St. Bernard of Clairvaux. 1090?-1153. French churchman; in 1115 he founded a Cistercian monastery at Clairvaux, where he remained as abbot for the rest of his life, refusing higher church offices; nevertheless, he was the most powerful figure in his day, becoming involved in many political affairs.

St. Carlo Borromeo. 1538-84. One of the leaders of the Counter Reformation, he played an important part in tthe Council of Trent, notably in drafting the Catechism. He organized the See of Milan.

St. Columba. 521-97. Irish missionary in Scotland. He went to Iona in 543 and established his center there, later converting the Scots to Christianity.

St. Filippo Neri. 1515-95. Born in Florence, St. Filippo Neri was a reformer and preacher to the poor. He encouraged popular devotion by means of religious songs and dramas set to music. The musical term "oratorio" is taken from St. Philip's Oratory in Rome.

St. Francis of Assisi (Francisco Bernadone). 1182?-1226. Founder of the Franciscan order, and one of the greatest of Christian saints. He gave up worldly things and preached and practised humility through joyful poverty, his singular devotion to mankind and his religious fervor. Stories of his life were collected in the *Little Flowers of St. Francis*.

St. Gregory of Tours. 538-94. Frankish bishop and historian.

St. Ignatius of Loyola. 1491-1556. Spanish by birth, St. Ignatius founded the Jesuit order. His *Spiritual Exercises* are reflections, examinations of conscience and prayers which form steps to mystical union with God. (see Jesuit order).

St. Jerome. c. 340-420. Christian ascetic and scholar. He was the chief translator of the Bible into the Vulgate, which became the authorized version of the Bible in the Catholic Church.

St. John of the Cross. 16th century. Spanish mystic and poet, student and associate of St.Theresa of Avila and founder of the men's order of Discalced (Barefoot) Carmelites. He wrote the mystical *Spiritual Canticle* (1577) in prison.

St. Just, Louis de. French revolutionist. 1767-94. Friend of Robespierre and a leading member of the Committee of Public Safety. Fanatically believed in the perfect state; active in overthrow of the Girondists and in bringing on the Reign of Terror. He was guillotined with Robespierre.

St. Longinus. Name traditionally given to soldier who pierced the side of Christ with his spear. Converted and martyred (according to *The Golden Legend*).

St. Theresa of Avila. 1515-82. The Spanish Carmelite nun, one of the principal saints of the Catholic Church, both practical manager and mystic. She founded the reformed Carmelite houses called Discalced (Barefoot). Mystical visions described in her *Life* (1562-65) were the subject of Bernini's masterpiece *The Ecstasy of St. Theresa*.

St. Thomas Aquinas. 1225-74. Italian philosopher, theologian. His major work is the *Summa theologica* (1267-73), an exposition of theology on rational principles. He was among the most brilliant of medieval scholastic philosophers.

Sassetta (Stefano di Giovanni). c. 1392-1450. A major Sienese 15th-century painter, he did not develop a realistic style but remained traditional. The best example of this is the altarpiece of St. Francis, painted for the church of San Francisco, Sansepolcro, now dispersed in several collections.

Savonarola, Girolamo. 1452-1498. Italian monk, reformer and martyr. Savonarola became a popular preacher, denouncing laxity with burning eloquence. When the Medici were exiled from Florence he became the virtual ruler, imposing a rigidly Puritan regime. After a conflict with the Pope was excommunicated, arrested and burned.

Schönborn Family. One of the few great families in Germany in the 17th and 18th centuries who were outstanding patrons of the arts. Lothar Francis Schönborn (1655-1729), bishop of Bamberg and elector of Mainz built the Residenz at Bamberg, the Favorite Palace at Mainz, and the palaces of Fulbach and Pommersfelden. Johann Philipp Franz, prince-bishop of Würzburg (1719-24) began the building of the Residenz at Würzburg, the most splendid residence in Germany. Friedrich Karl, bishop of Bamberg (1729-43), and from 1740 bishop of Konstanz, built the Palace of Bruchsal. Franz George, archbishop of Trier (1729-56), built the palaces of Trier and Koblenz. The architect of the Schönborn family was the great Balthasar Neumann, who developed a style which combined festive elegance and intense spirituality, and adapted Viennese and French influences.

Scott, Sir Walter. 1771-1832. Scottish poet, novelist, historian and biographer; remembered chiefly for long narrative poems with Gothic settings, such as *The Lady of the Lake* (1810) and for historical novels such as *Waverley* (1814) and *Ivanhoe* (1819).

Seurat, Georges. 1859-1891. French painter, originator of "pointillisme," in which light is rendered scientifically in touches of primary color as if seen through the spectrum.

Sforza, Francesco. 1401-66. Duke of Milan, 1450-66.

Shaftesbury, Anthony Ashley Cooper, seventh Earl of. 1801-85. English social reformer, parliamentary advocate of redressing the ills caused by the industrial revolution.

Shakespeare, William. 1564-1616. The greatest of English poets and dramatists, who produced comedies and tragedies as well as historical dramas. His sonnets are greatly admired for their lyricism and wit.

Shelley, Percy Bysshe. 1792-1822. English lyric poet whose political philosophy inspired radical thinkers.

Sixtus IV. 1414-84. Francesco della Rovere was pope from 1471-84. He commissioned the building of many of the palaces, churches and bridges of Rome. His greatest monument is the Sistine Chapel in the Vatican.

Sixtus V. 1521-90. Pope from 1585-90, Sixtus V was one of the great figures of the Catholic Reformation. He brought order to the Papal States and organized the pontifical administration. Sixtus spent vast revenues on the city to rebuild churches, redesign major streets and erect new buildings and monuments.

Smith, Adam. 1723-90. Scottish economist. His great work, *Inquiry into the Nature and Causes of the Wealth of Nations* (1776), laid the foundations of a science of political economy and set up a system of natural liberty of trade and commerce.

Spenser, Edmund. c. 1552-99. English poet of the Elizabethan period. Author of *The Faerie Queen,* one of the great English epic poems.

Sterne, Laurence. 1713-68. British author. An Anglican clergyman who published some sermons but is remembered for his worldly writing, notably *The Life and Opinions of Tristram Shandy* (1759-67), and *A Sentimental Journey through France and Italy* (1768). Sterne injected the sentimental novel with wit and charm.

Stubbs, George. 1724-1806. English painter of animals, who wrote *The Anatomy of the Horse,* 1766. In North Africa he saw a horse devoured by a lion and this vivid experience inspired a series of paintings which, in turn, influenced Delacroix.

Suger, Abbot. 1081-1151. Abbot of St. Denis, who rose from obscure origins to become a great monastic reformer and builder; built choir of St. Denis (1140-44), birthplace of Gothic style; served as regent of France (1147-49) while Louis VII led the Second Crusade.

Swift, Jonathan. 1667-1745. English satirist active in church, politics and literary circles. His most famous work, *Gulliver's Travels* (1726), satirizes the hypocrisy of courts, political parties and statesmen.

Talleyrand-Périgord, Charles Maurice de. 1754-1836. French statesman. Minister of foreign affairs under Napoleon; in 1814, instrumental in restoration of the Bourbons to the French throne, and became Louis XVIII's minister of foreign affairs; involved in Revolution of 1830, ambassador to Great Britain, 1830-34.

Tassie, James. 1735-99. Scottish gem engraver and modeler; executed large profile medallion portraits of his contemporaries.

Tennyson, Alfred, Lord. 1809-92. English Victorian poet; poet laureate after 1850. Among well-known works are "Locksley Hall," a religious poem, "Ulysses," "In Memoriam" and "The Charge of the Light Brigade."

Theodora. 508-48. Byzantine empress, consort of Justinian I.

Thomson, James. 1700-1748. English poet, born in Scotland. He wrote *The Seasons,* a long poem which describes the rural and urban activities of the four seasons and points a moral. His word pictures of weather and the times of day influenced English landscape painting.

Tiepolo, Giovanni Battista. 1696-1770. The last of the great Venetian decorators and the purest exponent of the Italian Rococo. Tiepolo created a world in steep perspective beyond the picture plane in his frescoes producing architecture that receded into dizzying distances. One of his most successful commissions was the ceiling of the Kaisersaal in the Residenz at Würzburg. The Prince-Bishop was so pleased that Tiepolo also painted the staircase with frescoes and some altarpieces.

Titian (Tiziano Vecelli). 1488/90-1576. Venetian painter, one of the main figures of Italian late Renaissance art. Painted religious altarpieces, mythological scenes and portraits of important persons in Europe. Among major works: *Assumption* (completed 1518), Pesaro Altar (1519-26), portraits of Pope Paul III and Emperor Charles V.

Tolstoy, Leo. 1828-1910. Russian novelist, protagonist of the people, in particular, the peasants. He initiated a cult of non-violence. He wrote *War and Peace,* which describes Napoleon's defeat by Russia's people and land, and *Anna Karenina.*

Troy, Jean François de. 1679-1752. French painter of historical and genre subjects.

Trumbull, John. 1756-1843. American painter of famous historical scenes, many of the American Revolution, and portraits.

Turner, Joseph Mallord William. 1775-1851. English landscape painter, best known for his seascapes. In his later works he painted the basic elements of nature—water, air, fire and snow.

Tyndale, William. c. 1482-1536. English religious reformer and translator of the Bible into English, which was later the basis for the King James version of the English Bible. Tyndale was condemned for heresy and put to death.

Urban VIII (Matteo Barberini). 1568-1644. Pope Urban VIII, 1623-44, patron of Bernini and Pietro da Cortona.

Vanbrugh, Sir John. 1664-1726. Architect and playwright, outstanding figure of the English Baroque period; commissioned by Queen Anne in 1705 to design Blenheim Palace, Oxfordshire. He and Nicholas Hawksmoor completed Wren's designs at Greenwich.

Van Eyck, Jan. 1390-1441. Flemish painter. Noted for realism imbued with mystical symbolism. He is credited with the invention of oil painting. Among major works: Ghent Altarpiece in St. Bavo, Ghent, Belgium, with brother Hubert.

Vanloo, Louis-Michel. 1707-71. French portrait painter, member of a family of painters descended from the Dutch painter Jan Vanloo (c. 1585-1630).

Vasari, Giorgio. 1511-1575. Florentine painter and art historian, whose Lives of the Most Excellent Architects, Sculptors and Painters is one of the major sources for Italian Renaissance artists and their works.

Vaughan, Henry. 1621-95. British metaphysical poet.

Velde, Willem I van de. 1611-93. His son, Willem. 1633-1707. Dutch artists who worked as official marine artists in England. Their records of sea-fights were done from drawings made under fire from a small boat in the thick of the action.

Vergil. 70-19 B.C. Roman poet, author of the Aeneid.

Vermeer, Jan, of Delft. 1632-75. Dutch painter of quiet domestic interiors. He studied the play of light and composed subtle designs with neatly balanced intervals.

Verrocchio, Andrea del. 1435-88. Florentine painter and sculptor. His workshop was a training center for young Florentine artists, notably Leonardo da Vinci.

Versailles. Begun 1669. Palace built for Louis XIV by Louis le Vau and J.-H. Mansart. Le Nôtre laid out the formal park and gardens.

Vesalius, Andreas. 1514-64. Flemish anatomist, whose discoveries, based on dissection, overthrew many doctrines of the Greek Galen (c. 130-c. 200), undisputed for fourteen centuries.

Vespasiano di Bisticci (Vespasiano Fiorentino). d. 1498. Scholar at the court of Federigo da Montefeltro, first Duke of Urbino; author of Vite di Uomini Illustri (Lives of Famous Men).

Vitruvius (Marcus Vitruvius Pollio). Late first century B.C. and early first century A.D. Roman writer on architecture; engineer and architect for the Roman Emperor Augustus; his theories were much used by architects of the classical revival during the Renaissance and the 18th century.

Voltaire (François Marie Arouet). 1694-1778. French philosopher, historian, writer and wit. His moral satire, Candide, derided the optimistic philosophy of the German philosopher Leibnitz. Famous for his defense of victims of religious intolerance. Spent last twenty years of his life (1758-78) at Ferney, near Geneva.

Wagner, Richard. 1812-83. German composer; based the librettos of his operas upon Germanic legend and literature. Most famous for his grand operas such as *Der Ring des Nibelungen* (1848-74), *Tannhauser* (1845) and *Tristan und Isolde* (1859).

Walton, Isaac. 1593-1683. English author who combined thought with fishing in *The Compleat Angler* (1653).

Watt, James. 1736-1819. Scottish mechanical engineer and inventor, invented the modern condensing steam engine which he manufactured with Matthew Boulton at Birmingham. Originated (with Boulton) the term horsepower. The watt, a unit of power, is named after him.

Wells, Herbert George. 1866-1946. English novelist, sociological writer and historian. Wrote many novels combining scientific speculation with social idealism, such as *The War of the Worlds* and *The Food of the Gods*.

Whitman, Walt. 1819-92. American poet. His *Leaves of Grass,* first published in 1855, is in free verse and celebrates love, mysticism, pantheism and democracy.

Wilberforce, William. 1759-1833. British statesman and abolitionist, parliamentary leader to outlaw the British slave trade. After its abolition in 1807 Wilberforce worked to eliminate slavery from the British Empire. The abolition law was passed one year after his death.

Wolf, Kaspar. 1735-98. Swiss painter of Alpine landscapes.

Wordsworth, Dorothy. 1771-1855. Devoted sister of the English poet William Wordsworth who lived with him in the Lake District and inspired much of his poetry. She wrote poetry and kept a journal about the Wordsworth household, friends and travels.

Wordsworth, William. 1770-1850. English poet, leader of the Romantic school in England. He wrote about the Lake District in northern England, his home, and about simple people. He saw nature as a moralizing and civilizing force.

Wren, Sir Christopher. 1632-1723. English architect and engineer. His opportunity came when the great fire of London, 1666, destroyed London. He built 51 parish churches in London, each one of a different design. His masterpiece, St. Paul's Cathedral, is a compromise between a Latin and Greek cross plan. He also designed the royal buildings at Greenwich: the Royal Observatory and Naval Hospital; their execution was left to his assistants at the Board of Works, John Vanbrugh and Nicholas Hawksmoor.

Wright of Derby (Joseph Wright). 1734-97. British painter who specialized in unusual lighting effects and moonlit landscapes. The industrialists Wedgwood and Arkwright were his patrons. He painted scientific experiments made by candlelight in the *Orrery* and *Experiment with an Air Pump.*

Yeats, William Butler. 1856-1939. Irish poet and dramatist whose better known poems include *Sailing to Byzantium* and *Galway Races.*

Zimmermann, Dominikus. 1685-1766. Bavarian architect and plaster worker who worked on several churches epitomizing the German Rococo style, notably the Wies church and the pilgrimage church of Steinhausen. Zimmerman is important for his contribution to church design on the oval plan and for adapting the French Rococo style to the heavier taste of southern Germany.

Zimmerman, Johann Baptist. 1680-1758. Bavarian skilled plasterer and painter who worked on the Munich Residenz and the Amalienburg under Cuvilliés. His brother Dominikus built the Wies church.

Geographical and Historical References

Aachen. A city in West Germany near the Dutch and Belgian borders, where Charlemagne built an elaborate palace and founded the cathedral that contains his tomb and that became the coronation place of German kings until 1531.

Aix-la-Chapelle. French name of Aachen (see above).

Apocalypse. A type of Hebrew and Christian inspired writing using veiled symbolism and prophesizing cosmic cataclysm.

Aqueduct. A structure that carries water, usually across a valley or over a river.

Assisi. Town in Umbria, central Italy. Birthplace of St. Francis, with many churches and a medieval atmosphere.

Barberini Palace, Rome, begun 1629 by Maderno for Pope Urban VIII, continued by Borromini and finished by Bernini. The ceiling of its Great Salon was painted by Pietro da Cortona (1633-39).

Bastille. Fortress and state prison located, until its demolition (1789-91), near the present Place de la Bastille, in Paris; detested symbol of the absolute power of the French monarchy, it was stormed by a Paris mob on July 14, 1789, now a national holiday.

Buckingham Palace. In London, residence of British sovereigns since 1837. Built in 1703 by the Duke of Buckingham on the site of a mulberry grove; purchased by George III in 1761 and remodelled repeatedly since.

Cambridge University. Cambridge, England. Founded in the early 12th century, it became a center of the new learning of the Renaissance and of the theology of the Reformation.

Carolingian. The arts, script and culture of the Frankish dynasty that reigned in France, 751-987, and in Germany until 911, characterized by a revival of classical forms modified by ecclesiastical dictates.

Carron works. Iron works in Stirlingshire, central Scotland. Founded c. 1760.

Celtic. Pertaining to a branch of Indo-European people and their languages which include Irish, Scots Gaelic, Welsh and Breton.

Cistercian Order. Founded by St. Robert at Cîteaux, Burgundy, 1090, in protest against the luxury of life and the extravagance of architectural decoration of the Cluniac order.

The City. A square mile in London on the north bank of the Thames, just west of the Tower and including St. Paul's Cathedral, the oldest part of

London, now the banking and commercial center of England. The parish churches in the City were designed by Wren.

Cluny. Town in central France which grew up around the abbey of Cluny, founded in 910.

Coalbrookdale. Iron works in western England established by Abraham Darby in 1708, where iron ore was first smelted with coke in 1709.

Commune of Paris. Extreme leftist government set up in Paris March-May, 1871, in wake of Franco-Prussian War, and ruthlessly put down with the execution of 17,000 people.

Conques. Town in southwest France, location of the Abbey of St. Foye.

Council of Trent. The ecumenical council of the Roman Catholic Church convoked to meet the crisis of the Protestant Reformation, 1545-47, 1551-52, 1562-63, by defining dogma and correcting abuses.

Crystal Palace. Constructed with prefabricated parts entirely of glass and iron, it could accommodate 250,000 visitors. Designed by Joseph Paxton for the Great International Exhibition of 1851.

Delos. A Greek island in the Cyclades in southwestern Aegean; site of an oracle of Apollo.

Encyclopédie. The work of the French Encyclopedists or *philosophes*—full title: *Encyclopédie; or Dictionnaire raisonné des sciences, des arts, et des métiers.*

Enlightenment. Term applied to the intellectual climate of 18th-century Europe, characterized by the *philosophes* (see above), who shared a belief in natural law, universal order, reason and human perfectability.

First Crusade. 1096-1099. Preached by Pope Urban II and led by French and Norman nobles; it captured Jerusalem in 1099.

Flanders. Former county in western Europe, extending along the North Sea from the Strait of Dover to the Schledt River; now divided between Belgium, France and the Netherlands.

Fountains Abbey. Ruined Cistercian abbey in Yorkshire, England (see Yorkshire).

Franconia. Medieval German duchy, a part of Bavaria 1806-15.

Franks. A Germanic people living along the Rhine. The Franks conquered Gaul 500 A.D., founded an extensive kingdom now called France.

French National Theater (Comédie Française). Most famous of the European state-subsidized theatres, organized in 1680. Housed in the Théatre Français, Paris, its repertory is based on the works of such classic French dramatists as Corneille, Racine, and Molière.

Gesù, Il. 1568-84. Chief Roman church of the Jesuit order. St. Ignatius of Loyola is buried there. Designed by Vignola and finished after 1573 by Giacomo della Porta, with illusionistic ceiling painted by Baciccio.

Girondiste. A political party in the French revolution. More moderate than the Jacobins who overthrew them and instigated the "Terror."

Grande Chartreuse. Carthusian monastery in the mountains near Grenoble, France.

Guild. Medieval association such as artisans and tradesmen organized to maintain standards of products and workmanship to protect the interests of its members and keep others from entering the trade, business, etc.

Grasmere. Village in the Lake District, northern England, where Wordsworth lived and wrote.

Great Ormond Street Hospital. Founded for sick children in the 19th century, later moved to Tadworth, Surrey, England. Shaftesbury was a founder, Dickens helped raise money.

Great Western Railway. Completed 1841, ran from Bristol to London.

Greenwich. Formerly village, now metropolitan borough of southeast London, on the Thames.

Haarlem. Capital of north Holland province, western Netherlands near the North Sea. The world tulip center since the 17th century and a center of 17th century Dutch painting.

Hanover, House of. European royal family which in 1714 inherited the British throne, in the person of George I (1714).

Hellebore. Name for winter or spring-blooming Eurasian perennial plants of genus *Helleborus,* of the buttercup family, used medicinally but highly toxic.

Hull. Town in Yorkshire, northern England. Home of William Wilberforce.

Humanist. One of the scholars of the Renaissance who studied the philosophy, history and culture of ancient Greece and Rome and applied this knowledge to a secular and critical study of the problems of his time.

Holy Roman Empire. Political conglomerate embracing most of central Europe from 962 to 1806. It claimed succession to imperial Rome and supremacy over Christendom. Its emperors were chosen by the Electors, princes of Germany.

Inquisition. A Roman Catholic tribunal for the discovery and punishment of heresy. Infamous for its torturing of accused and burning its victims at the stake (after 1250).

Iona. An island in the Hebrides, off the west coast of Scotland. The center of Celtic Christianity for four centuries after St. Columba came from Ireland in 543 to found the monastery which still stands and in which the *Book of Kells* was probably decorated.

Ionia. An ancient region on the west coast of Asia Minor and on adjacent islands in the Aegean, colonized by the ancient Greeks, flourished before the sixth century B.C. through the beginning of the Christian era. Birthplace of Ionian style of architecture and sculpture.

Islam. The religion of the Moslems, based on the words of the prophet Mohammed in the *Koran.*

Jesuit Order. A teaching order founded by St. Ignatius of Loyola to combat the Reformation, in 1540; the order freed its members from monasteries and urged active participation in the affairs of the world.

Koran. The sacred text of Islam believed to have been dictated to Mohammed by Gabriel; for Moslems, the foundation of law, religion, culture and politics.

La Grenouillère. On the Seine near Paris, popular river resort with boating, bathing and cafes, scene of paintings by Monet and Renoir.

Lake District. In northwest England, an area of lakes and low mountains. The home of Wordsworth and setting of much of his poetry.

Lindisfarne. An island off the coast of Northumberland in western England, the site of a Celtic monastery after which the famous seventh-century illuminated manuscript, the Lindisfarne Gospels, were named.

Manchester-Liverpool Railway, opened 1830. The first public railway on which all traffic was hauled by steam locomotives. An earlier railway line was Stockton-Darlington, 1825, which used horses as well as steam.

Mantua. Northern Italian town, in whose ducal palace Mantegna painted famous frescoes.

Marseillaise. The French national anthem written and composed by Claude Joseph Rouget de Lisle. Sung by a band of soldiers from Marseilles who marched on the Tuilleries on August 10, 1792, from that time known as the Marseillaise.

Missolonghi. City in west central Greece on the north shore of the Gulf of Patras. The Turks laid siege to Missolonghi in 1822-23 and in 1825-26. Byron died there in 1824.

Mull. An island in the Hebrides, near western Scotland.

Newgate. Notorious former prison in London, dating from the 12th century. Elizabeth Fry's reforms carried out there.

Nîmes. A town in the south of France, capital of the department of Gard and celebrated for its Roman ruins.

Norsemen. Ancient Scandinavians.

Nuremberg. City in central Bavaria in southeastern West Germany.

Old St. Peter's, Rome, 288?-337. The basilica was erected by Constantine near the site of the martyrdom of St. Peter. It was destroyed in 1505 by Pope Julius II to make way for the Renaissance basilica.

Ornans. Town in southeast France in which Gustave Courbet was born and where he painted.

Oxford University. Oxford, England. Originated in early 12th century. The university was a center of learning throughout the Middle Ages.

Padua. Town in northeastern Italy, near Venice.

Papal States. Former territory in Italy under the temporal rule of the popes.

Peasant's Revolt. 1524-26. General rising of German peasants against exploitation by the nobles. It was condemned by Martin Luther, and crushed by 1526, thus prolonging serfdom in Germany for almost three centuries and stunting democratic development.

Pilgrimage. A journey, especially a long distance, to some sacred place as an act of devotion.

Pistoia. Town in Tuscany, central Italy at foot of the Apennines.

Pyramid of Sakkara (Saqqara). Step-pyrmid of Zoser, built by Imhotep, in the third dynasty, 2650 B.C. Probably the oldest pyramid in Egypt.

Quakers, Society of Friends. Religious body originating in England in the 17th century under George Fox. The Quakers believed spiritual understanding could be found through "inward light." They refused to worship in established churches and to bear arms in war; they rejected social and official titles.

Quietism. Extreme form of mysticism proposed by the Spanish priest, Miguel de Molinos, and more moderately by French theologian Fénelon. Its essence is passivity before God for the sake of achieving unity with Him.

Reformation. The religious revolution in Western Europe in the 16th century which began as a reform movement in the Catholic church and led to the establishment of the Protestant churches.

Renaissance. The activity, spirit or time of the great revival of the arts and sciences in Europe during the 14th, 15th and 16th centuries. Originating in Florence, it was characterized by a rediscovery of classical culture, increased individualism and emphasis on worldly life.

"Rocket." The engine designed by George Stevenson that was the winner of the 1829 trials on the Liverpool-Manchester railway.

Royal Society of London for Improving Natural Knowledge, incorporated in the 1660's, founded to stimulate scientific discussion and research.

Sack of Rome, 1527. As a result of Pope Clement VII's alliance with Francis I, King of France, Rome was stormed and sacked (1527) by France's enemy, the Holy Roman Emperor Charles V.

St. Bartholomew's Day Massacre. Massacre by French catholics of Protestant leaders which began in Paris, August 24, 1572, and later spread into other sections of France, resulting in the resumption of civil religious wars.

San Ignazio, Rome. Begun 1626. Vast Jesuit church in Rome planned after the canonization of St. Ignazius. Illusionistic ceiling painted by Andrea Pozzo.

Sans Souci, Palace of, Potsdam. 1744-1747. Architect was Georg Wenceslaus von Knobelsdorff (1699-1753), built for Frederick the Great of Prussia.

Saracens. A term used in the Middle Ages to mean Arabs and, more generally, Moslems.

Sorbonne, University of the. First endowed college in the University of Paris, founded by Robert de Sorbon (1200-74); frequently used as a name for the University of Paris as a whole.

Styx. In classical mythology a river in the lower world over which the souls of the dead were ferried by Charon.

Tintern Abbey, ruined Cistercian abbey in western England. Subject of a poem by Wordsworth and of numerous paintings and etchings by 18th- and 19th-century English artists.

Trent. City in northern Italy (see Council of Trent).

University of Virginia. Located mainly at Charlottesville, Virginia, state-supported university chartered 1819, opened 1825 with Thomas Jefferson as its rector. Jefferson planned the curriculum and designed the original buildings.

Urbino. Town in central Italy (see Federigo da Montefeltro).

Valhalla. In Scandinavian mythology, the hall of immortality into which the souls of heroes slain in battle are received.

Vatican City. Independent sovereign state with the pope as its absolute ruler since 1929 and seat of the central government of the Roman Catholic Church. Includes the Cathedral of St. Peter's, the pontifical palaces and museum; has own coinage, postal system, diplomatic corps.

Vatican Library. The collection of ancient manuscripts that formed the nucleus of the library was begun while the popes were in Avignon. The library was greatly expanded by Popes Nicholas V (1447-55) and Sixtus IV (1471-84).

Vauxhall Gardens, London. The most celebrated of the pleasure gardens popular and fashionable from the 17th to 19th centuries.

Vézelay. Village in north-central France and site of Romanesque church of the Madeleine.

Vikings. Scandinavians pirates who plundered the northern and western coasts of Europe from the eighth to tenth centuries.

Weimar, Court of. Small principality in central Germany, known as a cultural center, which became the literary mecca of Germany when Goethe lived there, 1775-1832.

Wittenberg. City on the Elbe in east Germany which became a center of Lutheranism.

Yorkshire. County in northeast England.

Zeeland. A province in southwest Netherlands consisting mainly of islands.

Explanations of Special Words and Titles

Apse. A projecting part of a building, usually semicircular in plan and vaulted, appearing at the eastern, altar end of a church.

Baptistry. A separate building, chapel or part of a church reserved for the rites of baptism.

Barbarian style. A style originally developed by nomadic tribes in central Asia and later introduced by barbarian invaders into Europe; it is a decorative style, full of movement, with interlacing forms ultimately derived from animals and plants.

Baroque. A style of art of the 17th and earlier 18th centuries that originated in Italy and spread throughout Europe and to the New World, especially Mexico and South America; characterized by a sense of movement and a strong appeal to the emotions.

Basilica. (1) A type of building developed in classical Rome, with broad nave flanked by colonnaded aisles, ending in a semicircular apse. It was adopted as a typical church form in the Early Christian period. (2) Any Roman Catholic church which has been granted special ceremonial privileges.

Baldacchino. An ornamental structure over an altar.

Beehive huts. Small stone buildings, often circular in plan, roofed with stones, common to Celtic monasticism.

Byzantine. The style developed in the Byzantine Empire, largely in the fifth and sixth centuries, characterized by an ecclesiastically prescribed iconography, highly formal structure, severe confinement of pictorial space to a shallow depth and the use of rich colors.

Choir. In ecclesiastical architecture, the part of a church adjoining the altar and reserved for clergy.

Christmas Oratorio (1734), composed by Johann Sebastian Bach, with a text from verses in Luke and Matthew describing the Nativity.

Cistercian style. A severe and simple style of Gothic ecclesiastical architecture developed in the 11th century, characterized by lack of sculpture and stained glass ornament, and by the use of rectangular apses.

Classicism. A style of art derived from the study of antique precedents from Greece and Rome, characterized by idealized naturalism, symmetry and clarity.

Clerestory. An external wall of a building rising above adjoining roofs and pierced with windows.

Cloister. In ecclesiastical architecture, the covered, colonnaded walk surrounding an open court.

Cluniac style. Originating in the tenth century from the Abbey of Cluny, it is an ornate style of Romanesque architecture characterized by generous use of decoration, especially with painted sculpture, often including animals and monsters.

Cubism. A style of painting and sculpture developed in the early years of the present century by Picasso, Braque and others, and characterized by the abstraction of natural forms into angular elements.

Cupola. A cylindrical or polygonal roofed structure, pierced with windows, crowning a dome or roof.

Don Giovanni (1787), an opera in two acts by Wolfgang Amadeus Mozart. Libretto by Lorenzo da Ponte based on the Spanish Don Juan legend.

Early Christian art. That art which developed during the first three centuries of the Christian era.

Ecclesia. The Christian church often symbolized by the enthroned Madonna and Child.

Engraving. A method of printmaking in which lines, incised in a metal plate, retain the ink to transmit the design onto dampened paper under pressure; such a plate can produce innumerable prints.

Etching. Print-making in which the metal plate (often copper) is covered with a resinous ground impervious to acid. The etcher's needle exposes the metal wherever a line is wanted. Immersion of the plate in an acid bath eats away the exposed drawing on the plate. After inking, it is printed under pressure.

Facsimile. An exact copy, as of a book, painting or manuscript.

Flying buttress. An arch transmitting the outward and downward thrust of a wall, such as the outside wall of a church, to a vertical masonry support.

Font. A receptacle for baptismal or holy water in a church.

Frieze. A sculptured or otherwise ornamental horizontal band decorating a building.

Genre. Scenes of everyday life realistically rendered.

Gobelins. The state-controlled tapestry manufactory in Paris, founded as a dyeworks in the mid-15th century by Jean Gobelin.

Gothic. A style of architecture originating in France in the Paris area in the early 12th century and spreading throughout western Europe through the mid-16th century. It is characterized by the use of the pointed arch and the ribbed vault, and by a progressive lightening of the structural skeleton through the use of such features as flying buttresses.

Graeco-Roman. A style of art developed in the Roman Empire from the middle of the first century B.C. to the early fourth century A.D.; chiefly characterized by use of Greek formal motifs modified by technological innovation, monumental scale, and narrative treatment of subject matter.

Hellenistic. A term to describe the culture developed in Greece and the area conquered by Alexander the Great, from the end of the fourth to the first century B.C.; chiefly characterized by delicate and highly finished modeling, dramatic, often violent movement of forms in space, representations of extreme motion, individual characterization and widely varied subject matter.

High Renaissance. The highly developed style of Renaissance art occurring in Italy in the late 15th and early 16th centuries. The style is characterized by heroic proportions, idealized human forms and an appeal to intellect. Three giants of the High Renaissance were Leonardo, Michelangelo and Raphael.

Icelandic literature. The earliest literature of the Northmen, c. 850-1350, survives mainly in Icelandic vernacular writings. The most important work, the *Edda* (c. 800-1200), is a collection of lays about gods and heroes in old Icelandic mythology.

Illuminated manuscripts. Books handwritten on parchment or vellum and embellished with decorations in tempera, gold and occasionally silver.

Impressionism. A school of painting of the late 19th century in France, the first of the modern or non-academic movements. The Impressionists painted outdoors and studied the effect of light and color under different conditions. The first Impressionist exhibit, held in 1874, included Monet, Renoir, Sisley, Pissaro, Cézanne, Degas, Boudin, and Morisot.

Monasticism. A form of religious life lived according to strict rules based on chastity, obedience and poverty.

Mosaic. Decoration applied to floors, walls or vaults, made of small pieces of stone, glass, tile or other material inlaid in cement. Among the greatest examples are the Byzantine mosaics in the sixth century church of Santa Sophia in Constantinople and the several churches in Ravenna, Italy.

Mullion (also known as trumeau). A vertical member of stone or wood, between windows; in the Middle Ages a column, usually decorated, supporting the lintel of a doorway.

Nave. The central part of a church interior extending from entrance to altar.

Obelisk. A tapering, four-sided shaft of stone, terminating in a pointed or pyramidal top. In Egypt, obelisks were placed before temples and were usually incised with hieroglyphs.

Oratorio. Originally a religious counterpart to opera performed in the oratory of the Church of St. Philip at Rome, hence the name. There is no action or costumes but an emphasis on chorus and use of narrator.

Pericope. A section or extract from a book, especially from the Bible, chosen to be read in church or used as text for a sermon.

Perspective. A technique of depicting three-dimensional objects in spatial recession on a flat surface. All perspective systems assume that parallel lines never met but that they appear to do so. Perspective, as practiced now, is a sophisticated version of the system developed in the early 15th century in Italy.

Pilaster. A flat, rectangular, vertical, architectural feature projecting from a wall, having a capital and base imitating the form of a column.

Pointed arch. A curved masonry construction for spanning an opening, made up of a number of wedgelike stones, rising to a point at the apex; a typical feature of Gothic architecture.

Portico. A colonnaded, covered entrance to a building.

Reliquary. Shrine made to contain the relics of a saint.

Renaissance. The cultural movement which started in Florence in the early 15th century with a sudden rebirth of interest in the classical past and a deliberate attempt to recreate its spirit in contemporary form; the movement spread throughout Italy, then the rest of Europe; its art is characterized by a strong emphasis on realism, naturalism, humanism and individualism.

Rococo. A decorative, fanciful style of art which originated in France about 1700, and spread throughout Europe. It is characterized by intimacy of scale and the decorative use of asymmetrical arrangements of scrolls and counter-curves; Rococo painting was marked by lightness and gaiety.

Roman de la Rose, Le. French poem of 22,000 lines in two parts. The first written c. 1237 by Guillaume de Loris, is an allegory on the psychology of chivalric love. The second, written in 1275-80 by Jean de Meun, is satirical in tone and typifies the medieval bourgeois spirit.

Romanesque. A style of architecture which developed from the tenth to the 12th centuries in western and northern Europe, characterized by heavy masonry construction with narrow openings, use of round arch, barrel vault and the introduction and development of the vaulting rib, the vaulting shaft, and central and western towers for churches.

Romantic. A term used to describe the literary and artistic movements of the late 18th and early 19th centuries that revolted against the prescribed rules of classicism. It is characterized by interest in nature, in individualism, the emotional, the imaginative and the humanitarian.

Rose window. A circular window with metal-braced stone tracery supporting decorative glass used in medieval architecture.

Runic stones. Stones, often marking graves, incised with inscriptions in runes, characters of a northern Germanic alphabet used in Scandinavia and northern Europe from about the third to the 13th centuries.

Sacristy. The room, in or adjoining a church, in which sacred utensils and vestments are kept.

Saga. Originating in oral tradition, an epic narrative with historic or legendary elements, developed in ancient times in the Scandinavian north and later recorded.

St. Matthew Passion (The Passion according to St. Matthew), by Johann Sebastian Bach. It was sung in the Thomaskirche, Leipzig, on Good Friday, 1729. After Bach's death it was not performed until revived by Mendelssohn in Berlin in 1829.

Shaft. That part of a column or pier between the base and capitals. It supports, or seems to support, a vault or arch.

Sistine Chapel. The pope's private chapel in the Vatican, Rome, the ceiling and altar wall of which were painted by Michelangelo.

Tempera. Paint in which egg is used as the medium to bind the pigment usually to a prepared panel.

Troubadour poems. Poetry accompanied with music which flourished particularly in southern France from the 11th through the 13th centuries. Composed by aristocratic amateurs, its main theme is love.

Vault. An arched masonry covering, usually of stone in medieval architecture, to form a ceiling.

Woodcut. A printmaking technique in which that part of the design which is not to appear in the print is cut back from the surface of the wood block. Wood engraving is a more detailed medium in which the end-grain of the wood is engraved with the design.

Zwinger, Dresden. 1709-19. The Zwinger was a group of buildings, pavilions and screen-walls surrounding a court. It was commissioned by Augustus the Strong, King of Saxony, and designed by Matthaus Daniel Pöppelmann (1662-1736) as an open-air pleasure palace for court balls, plays and other entertainment.

Poetry

Program 1.

Unknown Anglo-Saxon poet, *The Wanderer.* Before 975.
Unknown Anglo-Saxon poet, *The Ruin.* Before 975.

Program 4.

W. B. Yeats, *A Wealthy Man who Promised a Subscription to the Dublin Gallery if it were Proved that People Wanted Pictures.* 1912.

Program 5.

William Shakespeare, *King Lear,* Act III, sc. 2, line 1. 1606.

Program 6.

William Shakespeare, *King Lear,* Act IV, sc. 6, line 154; *Macbeth,* Act V, Sc. 5, line 20. 1606; *Hamlet,* Act V, sc. 1, line 168. 1604.

Program 8.

Alexander Pope, *Epitaph on Newton.* 1727.
Henry Vaughan, *The World.* 1655.

Program 11.

William Collins, *Ode to Evening.* 1747.
Samuel T. Coleridge, *Hymn before Sunrise; The Vale of Chamonix.*

William Wordsworth, *The Excursion*, Book 4, 11. 978-985, 1814; *Lines Composed a Few Miles above Tintern Abbey, on Revisiting the Banks of the Wye During a Tour, July 13, 1798*, 11. 66-83; *The Tables Turned*, 1798; *The Sparrow's Nest*, 1801; *Tintern Abbey*, 11. 116-123; *Tintern Abbey*, 11. 100-102; *The Excursion*, Book 1, 11. 203-209.

Program 12.

Lord Byron, *Childe Harold's Pilgrimage*, Canto III, stanza 2, 1816.
Robert Burns, *For A' That*, 1795.
Thomas Osbert Mordaunt, *Verses Written During the War*, 1756-1763.
William Wordsworth, *The Prelude*, Book XI, 11. 106-109. 1799-1805.
William Wordsworth, *Prelude*, Book XI, 11. 141-143.
Lord Byron, *The Prisoner of Chillon*, section 14, 1816.
Lord Byron, *Childe Harold*, stanza 93, 1817.

Program 13.

Robert Burns, *On Carron Ironworks*, 1787.
Walt Whitman, *Song of the Broad-Axe*, part 9. 1856.
W. B. Yeats, *The Second Coming*, 1921 .

Music

The following is a listing of the musical selections used in the 13 programs of Kenneth Clark's "Civilisation" series. The recordings are listed in approximately the order in which they are heard in each film. An asterisk (*) before a selection indicates the recording used is currently available in the United States; when the recording used is not available but an alternative U.S. version exists, a dagger (†) precedes the listing. Out-of-print recordings are so indicated.

PROGRAM 1: The Frozen World

*Franck, Organ Chorale No. 3 in A Minor.
   Nicolas Kynaston playing the organ of Westminster Cathedral.
                                                              Odeon CSD-3648
*Messiaen, *Les Corps Glorieux:* "Combat de la mort et de la vie."
   Same performer as above.   Odeon CSD-3648
*Plainsong, *Quem quaeritis in sepulchro?*
   Brompton Oratory Choir conducted by Henry Washington.
                                                              RCA LM-6015
*Byzantine Hymn, *Ote to stavro*.
   Same performers as above.   RCA LM-6105
*Machaut, *Ma fin est mon commencement*.

Lemuel Hughes and Clarence Roberts with instrumental ensemble.
RCA LM-6016
Gregorian Chant, *Lumen ad revelationem—Nunc dimittis.*
Brompton Oratory Choir conducted by Henry Washington.
RCA LM-6015
Dunstable, *Veni Sancte Spiritus.*
Pro Musica Antiqua Ensemble conducted by Safford Cape.
RCA LM-6016
This program also includes some specially composed music by Edwin
Astley, performed by a group of musicians under the direction of Gerald
Jackson.

PROGRAM 2: The Great Thaw

Gregorian Chant, *Missa Solemnis Vespertina: In Cena Domini.*
Coro della Cappella Papale di San Francesco d'Assisi conducted by
Padre Maestro Alfonso del Ferraro. DG SLPM-139169 (out of print)
Anon., *Carmina Burana* (13th century anthology): "Fas et nefas ambu-
lant" and "Veris dulcis in tempore."
Members of the Studio der frühen Musik. Telefunken SAWT-9455
Gregorian Chant, *Cum natus esset Jesus; Kyrie fons bonitatis.*
Capella Antiqua of Munich conducted by Konrad Ruhland.
Telefunken SAWT-9493
Gregorian Chant, Mass for the Feast of the Assumption of the Blessed
Virgin Mary: The Gospel.
Nuns Choir of the Benedictine Abbey, Varensell.
DG Archive SAPM-198046 (out of print)
Gregorian Chant, First Mass for Christmas: Introit and Dominis Dixit.
Choir of the Monks of the Benedictine Abbey of Beuren conducted by
Pater Dr. Maurus Pfaff. DG Archive SAPM-198153

PROGRAM 3: Romance and Reality

Anon., *C'est la fin, Alta, Pour mon coeur, Novus miles sequitur, Ja nun
mons pris, Lamento di Tristan, Trotto.*
Gerald English (tenor) with the Jaye Consort conducted by Francis
Baines. Pye Golden Guinea GSGC-14092
Gregorian Chant, *O Redemptor sume carmen.*
Capella Antiqua of Munich conducted by Konrad Ruhland.
Telefunken SAWT-9493
Anon., *The Song of the Ass.*
Same performers as in anon. selections above.
Pye Golden Guinea GSGC-14092
Anon., Four 13th century dance tunes.
Carl Dolmetsch (recorder), Natalie Dolmetsch (viol), Donald Bridger
(English horn), Alan Taylor (tabor). RCA LM-6015

Anon., *Worldes Blis.*
Gerald English (tenor) with the Jaye Consort conducted by Francis Baines. Pye Golden Guinea GSGC-14092
*Dunstable, *Veni Sancte Spiritus.*
Pro Musica Antiqua Ensemble conducted by Safford Cape.
RCA LM-6016
This episode also includes plainsong recorded on location at Chartres by the boys' choir of the cathedral.

PROGRAM 4: Man—the Measure of All Things

Jannequin, *Martin* (for 2 trumpets and 2 trombones).
Roger Blanchard Instrumental Ensemble.
HMV HQS-1044 (out of print)
*Queldryke, *Gloria in excelsis.*
Ambrosian Singers conducted by Denis Stevens. Odeon CSD-3504
*Dufay, *In tempore Passionis.*
Choir of the Carmelite Priory conducted by John McCarthy.
Everest 3174
*Josquin des Prez, *Ave verum Corpus natum.*
Capella Antiqua of Munich conducted by Konrad Ruhland.
Telefunken SAWT-9480
Isaac, *Sempre giro piangendo.*
Friedrich Schmidtmann (recorder), Eugen Müller-Dombois and Michael Schäffer (lutes). Angel S-36379 (out of print)
*Anon., *La Spagna.*
Zurich Ensemble of Ancient Instruments. Odyssey 32160036
*Landini, *Gram piant'agli occhi.*
Members of the Studio der frühen Musik. Telefunken SAWT-9466
*Anon., *Mij quam eyn hope.*
Same performers as above. Telefunken SAWT-9432
*Landini, *Ecco la primavera.*
Same performers as above. Telefunken SAWT-9466
*Anon., *Très douce regard.*
Same performers as above. Telefunken SAWT-9466
Jannequin, *Chantons, sonnons, trompettes.*
Roger Blanchard Instrumental Ensemble.
HMV HQS-1044 (out of print)
*Lapaccino, *Se me grato.*
Members of the Studio der frühen Musik. Telefunken SAWT-9466
*Filismo, *L'amor donna.*
Same performers as above. Telefunken SAWT-9466
*Anon., Two pavanes.
Zurich Ensemble of Ancient Instruments. Odyssey 32160036
*Josquin des Prez, *La Deploration de Johann Okeghem.*
Choir of the Carmelite Priory conducted by John McCarthy.
Everest 3174

*Anon., *Venid a sospirar.*
Members of the Studio der frühen Musik.   Telefunken SAWT-9432

PROGRAM 5: The Hero as Artist

†Giovanni Gabrieli, *Canzona primi toni.*
Philadelphia Brass Ensemble, Cleveland Brass Ensemble, Chicago Brass
Ensemble.   Columbia MS-7209
Isaac, *An buos.*
Vienna Concentus Musicus conducted by Nikolaus Harnoncourt.
DG Archive SAPM-198323 (out of print)
*Victoria, Responsaries for Tenebrae: Holy Saturday, Third Nocturn,
No. 2 "Aestimatus sum."
Westminster Cathedral Choir conducted by George Malcolm.
Argo ZRG-5149
Isaac, *Proprium Missae in Dominica Laetare.*
Aachen Cathedral Choir conducted by Theodor B. Rehmann.
DG EPA-37094 (out of print)

PROGRAM 6: Protest and Communication

*Tomkins, Voluntary.
Christopher Gower (organ).   Argo ZRG-5249
Demantius, *Ich bin ein guter Hirt.*
Mannheim Youth Choir conducted by Rolf Schweizer.
Musica Rara MUS-26
†Dowland, *Melancholy Galliard.*
Julian Bream (lute).   Westminster W-9079
*Farnaby, *Tell me, Daphne.*
Thurston Dart (harpsichord).   Oiseau-Lyre OL-50131

PROGRAM 7: Grandeur and Obedience

†Monteverdi, *L'Orfeo:* Toccata.
Vienna Concentus Musicus conducted by Nikolaus Harnoncourt.
Telefunken SKH-21
Gregorian Chant, Mass for the Feast of the Assumption of the Blessed
Virgin Mary.
Nuns of the Benedictine Abbey, Varensell.
DG Archive SAPM-198046 (out of print)
*Giovanelli, *Nunc Dimittis.*
Capella Antiqua of Munich conducted by Konrad Ruhland.
Telefunken SAWT-9456
*Monteverdi, *Vespro della Beata Vergine:* Domine et advisovadum, Nisi
Dominus, Magnificat, Sonata sopra Maria pro nobis, Dixit Dominus.
Soloists, Vienna Boys' Choir, Monteverdi Choir of Hamburg and Vienna

Concentus Musicus conducted by Jürgen Jürgens, with the Schola Cantorum of the Capella Antiqua of Munich.

Telefunken SAWT-9501/2

*Giovanni Gabrieli, *Jubilate Deo.*
Capella Antiqua of Munich conducted by Konrad Ruhland.

Telefunken SAWT-9456

†Giovanni Gabrieli, *Canzona primi toni.*
Philadelphia Brass Ensemble, Cleveland Brass Ensemble, Chicago Brass Ensemble.　　　　　　　　　　　　　　　　Columbia MS-7209

PROGRAM 8: The Light of Experience

*D'Anglebert, *Le Tombeau de M. de Chambonnières.*
Gustav Leonhardt (harpsichord).　　　　RCA Victrola VICS-1370
†Praetorius, Dances from *Terpsichore:* Entrée.
Collegium Terpsichore.　　　　　　　DG Archive SAPM-198166
　Froeberger, *Lamento.*
Lionel Rogg (harpsichord).　　　　　　　　　　Oryx 711
*Purcell, *Dido and Aeneas:* Act 3 (Sailor's Song).
St. Anthony Singers and English Chamber Orchestra conducted by Anthony Lewis.　　　　　　　Oiseau-Lyre SOL-60047
*Purcell, Sonata for Trumpet and Strings.
Dennis Egan (trumpet), the Philomusica of London conducted by Anthony Lewis.　　　　　　　Oiseau-Lyre SOL-60002
*Purcell, *The Gordian Knot Untied:* Overture.
Prague Chamber Orchestra.　　　　　　　　Artia ALPS-194

PROGRAM 9: The Pursuit of Happiness

†Handel, Concerto Grosso, Op. 3, No. 3: First Movement.
Academy of St. Martin-in-the-Fields conducted by Neville Marriner.

Argo ZRG-5400

*Bach, *St. Matthew Passion:* No. 67 (Recitative and Chorus).
Peter Pears (tenor), Stuttgart Hymnus Choir, Stuttgart Chamber Orchestra conducted by Karl Münchinger.　　　London CSA-1431
*Bach, *Christmas Oratorio:* Opening chorus.
Lübecker Kantorei, Stuttgart Chamber Orchestra conducted by Karl Münchinger.　　　　　　　　　　London CSA-1386
†Buxtehude, Toccata and Fugue in F Major.
E. Power Biggs playing the organ of the Johanneskirche, Lüneberg.

Columbia MS-6944

*Handel, *Alcina:* "Questo è il cielo discontenti."
Graziella Sciutti (soprano), London Symphony Orchestra and Chorus conducted by Richard Bonynge.　　　　London OSA-1361
†Handel, *Messiah:* "I Know that my Redeemer Liveth."

Heather Harper (soprano), the London Symphony Orchestra conducted by Colin Davis. Philips PHS-900214

Francisque (transcribed Grandjany), Prelude and Bransles.
Marisa Robles (harp). Argo ZRG-5458

Haydn, String Quartet in G Major, Op. 77, No. 1: First Movement.
Amadeus String Quartet. DG SLPM-138980

Haydn, *The Creation:* Part 3, Duet of Adam and Eve.
Agnes Giebel (soprano), Gottlob Frick (bass), the Bavarian Radio Choir and Symphony Orchestra conducted by Eugen Jochum.
Philips PHS 2-903

Mozart, String Quartet in G Major (K. 387): Fourth Movement.
Amadeus String Quartet. DG SLPM-138909

Mozart, *Don Giovanni:* Act 1, Scene 1.
Joan Sutherland (soprano), Eberhard Wächter (baritone), Giuseppe Taddei and Gottlob Frick (basses), the Philharmonia Orchestra conducted by Carlo Maria Giulini. Angel SD-3605

The scene shown in this program is taken from the Paul Czinner film of the 1954 Salzburg Festival production with Elisabeth Grümmer (soprano), Cesare Siepi, Otto Edelmann and Deszö Ernster (basses) and the Vienna Philharmonic Orchestra conducted by Wilhelm Furtwängler.]

PROGRAM 10: The Smile of Reason

*Mozart, String Quintet in E Flat Major (K. 614): Third Movement.
The Heutling Quartet with Heinz-Otto Graf (viola).
Seraphim SIC-6028

†Handel, *Music for the Royal Fireworks*: Minuet II.
Band of 64 Winds and 9 Percussion conducted by Charles Mackerras.
Vanguard Everyman SRV-289 SD

*Mudge, Concerto No. 1 in D Major.
Maurice André (trumpet), the Oiseau-Lyre Ensemble conducted by Pierre Columbo. Oiseau-Lyre OL-50137

*Gay-Pepusch, *The Beggar's Opera:* "In the days of my youth . . ."
Marjorie Westbury (contralto) with the Argo Ensemble conducted by Richard Austin. Argo DA-10/11

*Lully (arr. Koschinsky), Suite *Musiciens du roi*: Fanfare.
Prague Chamber Orchestra. Artia ALPS-194

*Mozart, Piano Quartet in G Minor (K. 478): Third Movement.
Peter Serkin (piano), Alexander Schneider (violin), Michael Tree (viola), David Soyer (cello). Vanguard Everyman SRV-284 SD

* Anon., *Will ye go to Sheriffmuir?*
Ewen Maccoll accompanied by Peggy Seeger. Folkways 8756

*Hewitt, *The Battle of Trenton.*
E. Power Biggs (organ). Columbia MS-6161

*Ives, Variations on *America.*
E. Power Biggs (organ). Columbia MS-6161

PROGRAM 11: The Worship of Nature

*Beethoven, Concerto in C Major for Violin, Cello, Piano and Orchestra, Op. 56: Second Movement.
Wolfgang Schneiderhan (violin), Pierre Fournier (cello), Geza Anda (piano) with the Berlin Radio Symphony Orchestra conducted by Ferenc Fricsay.   DG SLPM-136236
*Brahms, Concerto in A Minor for Violin, Cello and Orchestra, Op. 102: Second Movement.
Josef Suk (violin), André Navarra (cello) with the Czech Philharmonic Orchestra conducted by Karel Ancerl.   Parliament ALPS-601
†Schubert, Quintet in A Major for Piano and Strings, D. 667 (*The Trout*): Second Movement.
Christoph Eschenbach (piano) and the Koeckert Quartet.
                                                                     DG SLPM-136488
*Brahms, *Tragic Overture*, Op. 81.
Czech Philharmonic Orchestra conducted by Karel Ancerl.
                                                                     Parliament ALPS-601
†Debussy, *Nocturnes:* "Nuages."
The Philharmonia Orchestra conducted by Carlo Maria Giulini.
                                                                         Angel S-35977
*Debussy, *La Mer:* "De l'aube à midi sur la mer."
L'Orchestre de la Suisse Romande conducted by Ernest Ansermet.
                                                                        London CS-6437

PROGRAM 12: The Fallacies of Hope

*Tchaikovsky, *Francesca da Rimini:* Beginning.
New York Stadium Symphony Orchestra conducted by Leopold Stokowski.   Everest SDBR-3011
*Beethoven, *Leonore Overture* No. 3, Op. 72a.
Israel Philharmonic Orchestra conducted by Lorin Maazel.
                                                                        London CS-6328
*Rouget de Lisle, *La Marseillaise*.
Red Army Ensemble conducted by Boris Alexandrov.   Angel S-36206
*Anon., Fanfare *Le Champ d'Honneur*.
Brass and Percussion Ensembles of the Paris Gardiens de la Paix conducted by Désiré Dondeyne.   Nonesuch H-71075
*Beethoven, Symphony No. 3 in E Flat Major, Op. 55 (*Eroica*): Second Movement.
Berlin Philharmonic Orchestra conducted by Herbert von Karajan.
                                                                      DG SLPM-138802
*Beethoven, *Fidelio:* Prisoners' Chorus.
Vienna State Opera Chorus, Vienna Philharmonic Orchestra conducted by Lorin Maazel.   London OS-26009
†Berlioz, *King Lear*, Op. 4.
London Symphony Orchestra conducted by Colin Davis.
                                                                  Philips PHS-900138

*Richard Strauss, Festive Prelude for Organ and Orchestra.
  Wolfgang Meyer (organ), Berlin Philharmonic Orchestra conducted
  by Karl Böhm.   DG SLPM-138866
*Richard Strauss, *Till Eulenspiegel.*
  Berlin Philharmonic Orchestra conducted by Karl Böhm.
                                                   DG SLPM-138866

PROGRAM 13: Heroic Materialism

---

†Walton, Symphony No. 1 in B flat minor: First Movement.
  London Symphony Orchestra conducted by André Previn.
                                                   RCA LSC-2927
*Eduard Strauss, *Bahn Frei* (Polka Galop), Op. 45.
  Vienna Philharmonic Orchestra conducted by Willi Boskovsky.
                                                   London CS-6340
†Offenbach, *La Belle Hélène*: Overture (waltz tune).
  L'Orchestre de la Suisse Romande conducted by Ernest Ansermet.
                                                   London CS-6205
*Britten, *Spring Symphony*, Op. 44: "Shine Out" and "The Driving Boy."
  Peter Pears (tenor), Jennifer Vyvyan (soprano), Norma Proctor (con-
  tralto), the Royal Opera House, Covent Garden, Chorus and Orchestra
  conducted by Benjamin Britten.   London OS-25242
*Victoria, Responsaries for Tenebrae: Holy Saturday, Third Nocturn, No.
  2 "Aestimatus Sum."
  Westminster Cathedral Choir conducted by George Malcolm.
                                                   Argo ZRG-5149
†Stravinsky, *Apollo*: Coda.
  Columbia Symphony Orchestra conducted by Igor Stravinsky.
                                                   Columbia MS-6466

Reading List

The Reading List has been compiled with emphasis on works in print
and on those available in paperback (designated with an asterisk).
The many volumes of the *Pelican History of Art* (Penguin Books, Baltimore) admirably cover most aspects of Western art; the *Encyclo-
pedia of World Art* (15 volumes, McGraw-Hill, Institutio per la Col-
laborazione Culturale), also available in many libraries, is another
detailed source. The *Time-Life Library of Art* contains well-illustrated
works on individual artists while the *Great Ages of Man* series pro-
vides useful background. Prentice-Hall's volumes of *Sources and Do-
cuments in the History of Art* are also valuable. E. Louise Lucas's *Art
Books: A Basic Bibliography on the Fine Arts** (New York Graphic

Society) is a classic list. More specialized references may be found in most of the works included below.

A. General

Andrews, Wayne, *Architecture, Ambition and Americans: A Social History of American Architecture. Free Press, 1964. Amusing, readable.

Clark, Kenneth. *The Nude: A Study of Ideal Form. Anchorage, Doubleday, 1956. Readable study of an important subject.

Cleaver, Dale. *Art: An Introduction. Harcourt Brace & World, 1966. A useful, brief introduction.

Einstein, Alfred. *A Short History of Music. Vintage, Random House, 1954.

Gardner, Helen. Art Through the Ages, 5th ed. Harcourt Brace Jovanovich, 1970. An excellent survey.

Grout, Donald J. History of Western Music, Shorter Edition. Norton, 1964.

Holt, E. G., ed. *Documentary History of Art, 2 vols. Anchorage, Doubleday, 1966. Immensely informative.

Ivins, Williams, Jr. *How Prints Look. Beacon Press, 1958. Excellent.

Janson, H. W. History of Art, revised edition. Abrams, 1969. An excellent survey.

Jordan, Robert Furneaux. *A Concise History of Western Architecture. Harcourt Brace Jovanovich, 1970. Excellent, brief survey.

McLanathan, Richard. *The American Tradition in the Arts. Harcourt Brace & World, 1968. A selective interpretative survey.

Museums Directory of the United States and Canada. American Association of Museums, Washington, D.C., 1969. A useful reference for the nature of collections.

Pevsner, Nikolaus. *An Outline of European Architecture. 6th Jubilee edition. Penguin, 1960. Good survey.

Rasmussen, S. E. *Experiencing Architecture, 2nd edition. MIT Press.

Schevill, Ferdinand. History of Europe from the Reformation to the Present Day, revised edition. Harcourt Brace & World, 1957.

Stevens, Denis and Alec Robertson. *The Pelican History of Music, 3 vols. Penguin, 1962.

B. The Ancient World

Brown, Frank E. *Roman Architecture. Braziller, 1961.

Groenewegen-Frankfort, H. and Bernard Ashmole. *The Ancient World. New American Library, 1967.

Richter, Gisela M. A. Handbook of Greek Art, 6th edition. Phaidon, London, 1969.

Scranton, Robert L. *Greek Architecture. Braziller, 1962.

Wheeler, Mortimer. *Roman Art and Architecture. Praeger, 1966.

C. The Middle Ages

Adams, Henry. *Mont Saint-Michel and Chartres, many editions. A thoughtful readable classic.

Barraclough, Geoffrey. *Medieval Papacy. Harcourt Brace & World, 1968.

Beckwith, John. *The Art of Constantinople,* 2nd edition. Praeger, 1968.

Evans, Joan. *Art in Medieval France.* Oxford University Press, New York, 1948.

Grivot, Denis, and George Zarnecki. *Gislebertus, Sculptor of Autun.* Orion, 1961. A beautiful book on a great medieval sculptor.

Harvey, John H. *The Gothic World, 1100-1600.* Harper & Row. Especially strong in British architecture.

Henry, Françoise. *Irish Art during the Viking Invasions A.D. 800-1020.* Cornell University Press, 1967. By the leading authority in the field.

———. *Irish Art in the Early Christian Period, to 800 A.D.* Cornell University Press, 1965.

Hinks, Roger P. *Carolingian Art.* University of Michigan Press, 1962. Brief readable account.

Jantzen, Hans. *High Gothic: The Classic Cathedrals of Chartres, Reims and Amiens.* Minerva; Funk and Wagnalls, 1962.

McLanathan, Richard. *Pageant of Medieval Art and Life.* Westminster, 1966. Brief readable survey of entire period.

Martindale, Andrew. *Gothic Art.* Praeger, 1967.

Mâle, Emile. *Gothic Image: Religious Art in France of the Thirteenth Century.* Torchbooks; Harper & Row, 1958. Basic work by a leading scholar.

———. *Religious Art: From the Twelfth to the Eighteenth Century.* Page; Farrar, Straus & Giroux.

Morey, Charles R. *Christian Art.* Norton, 1962.

———. *Medieval Art.* Norton, 1942. Still the classic text.

Moss, H. S. *The Birth of the Middle Ages, 395-814.* Oxford University Press, 1963.

Power, Eileen. *Medieval People,* 10th revised and enlarged edition. Everyday Handbooks; Barnes & Noble. Lively accounts of lives of people from different walks of life.

Ross, James B. and Mary McLaughlin, eds. *Portable Medieval Reader.* Viking Press, 1949. Well selected, readable.

Runciman, Steven. *A History of the Crusades,* 3 vols. Cambridge University Press, 1951-54. The classic work on the subject.

Stoddard, Whitney. *Monastery and Cathedral in France.* Wesleyan University Press, Middletown, Conn., 1966. Scholarly, definitive.

Swarsenski, Hans. *Monuments of Romanesque Art: The Art of Church Treasuries in North-Western Europe,* 2nd edition. University of Chicago Press, 1967.

Talbot Rice, David. *The Art of the Byzantine Era.* Praeger, 1963.

———. *Islamic Art.* Praeger, 1965.

Temko, Allan. *Notre Dame of Paris.* Viking Press. Readable, lively, fascinating.

Trevor-Roper, Hugh. *The Rise of Christian Europe.* Harcourt Brace & World, 1965.

Volbach, Wolfgang Fritz. *Early Christian Art.* Abrams, 1962. Good survey.

Wallace-Hadrill, J. M. *The Barbarian West: The Early Middle Ages A.D. 400-1000.* Torchbook; Harper & Row.

D. The Renaissance and the Baroque

Bazin, Germain. *Baroque and Rococo Art. Praeger, 1964.

Berenson, Bernard. *Italian Painters of the Renaissance, 2 vols. Praeger; Phaidon, 1967. Classic work by a famous scholar and personality.

Burckhardt, Jacob. *The Civilization of the Renaissance in Italy, 2 vols. Torchbook; Harper & Row, 1960. A classic work by the scholar who virtually rediscovered the Renaissance.

Châtelet, Albert and Jacques Thuillier. French Painting, 2 vols. Skira, 1962.

Clark, Kenneth, *Leonardo da Vinci. Pelican; Penguin, 1939. Thoughtful treatment of Leonardo as a painter.

Cuttler, Charles. Northern Painting from Pucelle to Bruegel. Holt Rinehart Winston, 1968.

De Tolnay, Charles. Michelangelo, 5 vols. Princeton University Press, 1943-60. The classic major work.

Frame, Donald M. Montaigne. Harcourt Brace & World, 1965.

Friedlander, Max J. *From Van Eyck to Bruegel: Early Netherlandish Painting, 3rd edition. Praeger, 1969. Work of a leading scholar in the field.

Hartt, Frederick, The History of Italian Renaissance Art. Abrams, 1969. Solid reference work.

Hazard, Paul. *European Thought in the Eighteenth Century from Montesquieu to Lessing. Meridian; World Publishing, 1954.

Hind, Arthur M. *History of Engraving and Etching, 3rd revised edition, reprinted, Dover. The best survey so far.

———. *An Introduction to a History of Woodcut, 2 vols. Reprinted, Dover.

McLanathan, Richard. Images of the Universe: Leonardo da Vinci, the Artist as Scientist. Doubleday, 1968.

Panofsky, Erwin. Albrecht Dürer, 3rd edition, 2 vols. Princeton University Press, 1948. A distinguished work by one of the greatest scholars of our century.

Portoghesi, Paolo. The Rome of Borromini. Braziller, 1968.

Rosenberg, Jakob. *Rembrandt, Life and Works, revised edition. Phaidon; Praeger, 1964. The most complete brief work on the subject.

Schevill, Ferdinand. *The Medici. Torchbook; Harper & Row, 1960.

Shearman, John. *Mannerism: Style and Civilization. Pelican; Penguin, 1967.

Stechow, Wolfgang. Dutch Landscape. Painting of the Seventeenth Century, revised edition. Phaidon, 1966.

Vasari, Giorgio. *The Lives of the Painters, Sculptors and Architects, translated by A. M. Hind, 4 vols. Many editions. A basic contemporary source, gossipy and admiring.

Wittkower, Rudolf. Sculptures of Bernini, revised edition. Praeger, 1966.

E. Later Eighteenth Century and the Modern World

Barr, Alfred H., Jr., ed. *What is Modern Art?* Museum of Modern Art, New York, 1951.

Behrens, C. B. A. *The Ancien Régime.* Harcourt Brace Jovanovich, 1970.

Brion, Marcel. *Art of the Romantic Era: Romanticism, Classicism, Realism.* Praeger, 1966.

Brown, Milton W. *American Painting from the Armory Show to the Depression.* Princeton University Press, 1955.

Elsen, Albert. *Rodin.* Distributed by NYGS, Museum of Modern Art, New York, 1963. The best work on Rodin so far, though limited in scope.

Friedlaender, Walter F. *From David to Delacroix.* Reprinted, Schocken, 1952.

Gay, Peter. *Voltaire's Politics: The Poet as Realist.* Reprinted, Random House, 1965.

Hamlin, Talbot. *Greek Revival Architecture in America.* Reprinted, Dover, 1944. The best book on the subject.

Hampson, Norman. *The First European Revolution 1776-1815.* Harcourt Brace Jovanovich, 1970.

Hatton, Ragnhild N. *Europe in the Age of Louis XIV.* Harcourt Brace Jovanovich, 1970.

Henderson, W. O. *Industrialization of Europe: 1780-1914.* Harcourt Brace & World, 1969.

Larkin, Oliver. *Art and Life in America,* revised edition. Holt Rinehart Winston, New York, 1960. A detailed compendious survey.

Read, Herbert. *A Concise History of Modern Sculpture.* Praeger, 1964.

––––. *A Concise History of Modern Painting.* Praeger, 1964. Both brief, excellent.

Rewald, John. *History of Impressionism,* revised edition. Museum of Modern Art, New York, 1962. A classic work by a leading expert.

––––. *History of Post-Impressionism from Van Gogh to Gauguin.* Museum of Modern Art, New York, 1962.

Richardson, Edgar P. *Painting in America: From 1502 to the Present.* Crowell, 1965.

Talmon, J. L. *Romanticism and Revolt: Europe 1815-48.* Harcourt Brace Jovanovich, 1970.

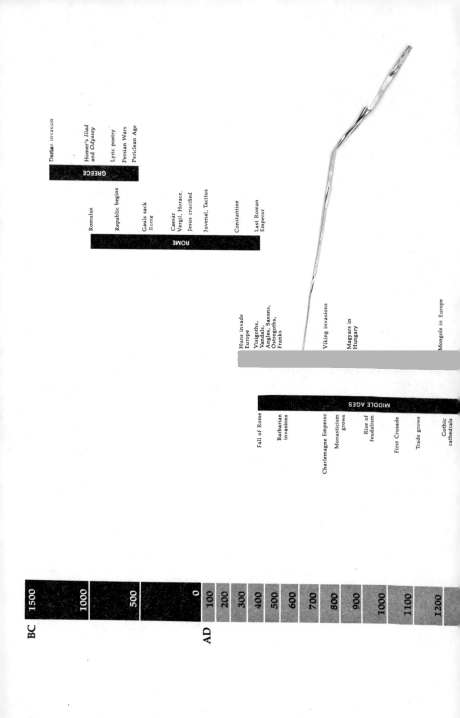

BC
1500
1000
500

AD
0
100
200
300
400
500
600
700
800
900
1000
1100
1200

GREECE

Dorian invasion
Homer's *Iliad and Odyssey*
Lyric poetry
Persian Wars
Periclean Age

ROME

Romulus
Republic begins
Gauls sack Rome
Caesar
Vergil, Horace, Jesus crucified
Juvenal, Tacitus
Constantine
Last Roman Emperor

Huns invade Europe
Visigoths, Vandals, Angles, Saxons, Ostrogoths, Franks
Viking invasions
Magyars in Hungary
Mongols in Europe

MIDDLE AGES

Fall of Rome
Barbarian invasions
Charlemagne Emperor
Monasticism grows
Rise of feudalism
First Crusade
Trade grows
Gothic cathedrals

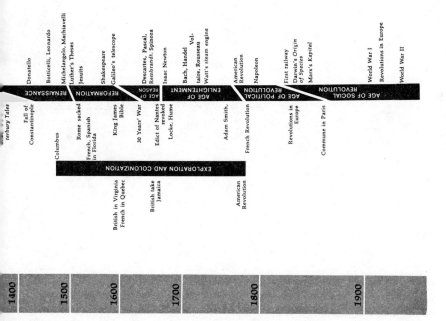

The duration of historical periods can be reckoned by reference to the time bar at far left. This bar is calibrated according to a logarithmic formula which enables the space allotted to each century to become progressively greater as it approaches the present. As a result, there is a deliberate distortion to compress the material within the available space and to allow for the greater knowledge of more recent eras.

Time bar: 1400 — 1500 — 1600 — 1700 — 1800 — 1900

Period bars: RENAISSANCE · REFORMATION · AGE OF REASON · AGE OF ENLIGHTENMENT · AGE OF POLITICAL REVOLUTION · AGE OF SOCIAL REVOLUTION · EXPLORATION AND COLONIZATION

Events above the bar:
Donatello · Botticelli, Leonardo · Michelangelo, Machiavelli · Luther's Theses · Jesuits · Shakespeare · Galileo's telescope · Descartes, Pascal, Rembrandt; Spinoza · Isaac Newton · Bach, Handel · Voltaire, Rousseau · Watt's steam engine · American Revolution · Napoleon · First railway · Darwin's Origin of Species · Marx's Kapital · World War I · Revolutions in Europe · World War II

Events below the bar:
...terbury Tales · Fall of Constantinople · Columbus · Rome sacked · French, Spanish in Florida · King James Bible · 30 Years' War · Edict of Nantes revoked · Locke, Hume · Adam Smith · French Revolution · Revolutions in Europe · Commune in Paris · British in Virginia · French in Quebec · British take Jamaica · American Revolution